The Day After the

End of the World

A tale of catastrophe and other gifts

Rebecca Long Howard

The Day After the

End of the World

DEDICATION

O Best Beloved, my life began in the moment I met you. You are my heart, my hero, and my joy. Thank you for changing my name to Mom.

Froggie, you are the rare creature who improves the entire universe, simply by existing. You are my sunshine.

In Memory of Bruce: Yes, sir, best friends. Always and always and always.

CONTENTS

INTRODUCTION

Home, the Original

If home is where you hang your heart, then for a quarter century, I went without so much as a place to put the nail. Childhood with a single parent involved packing up every few years. Home was always my mother and brother, never the current roof over our heads. Though I always had a weekend room at my father's house, it was simply a place to sleep, or more often, to read of places I would rather be. Regardless of my location, I wanted to be somewhere else, not through dissatisfaction or unhappiness; time to move on just seemed to come quickly for me.

At sixteen, I moved from the place of childhood and began my one permanent vocation, motherhood. After a brief marriage, through circumstance and decision, my son and I wandered. Every couple of years, I would load up my little blue-eyed soul and thrift store furniture, and take off for the perpetual Elsewhere.

I decided that though my son knew he could always count on Mama's presence, he also needed roots, a single place to grow up stable and strong. When he was seven, his gypsy Mama, armed with a growing list of pros and cons, went house hunting.

I was not looking for anything permanent, merely a safe place to raise my kid for the span of a single childhood, when an inexplicable sensation met me in the driveway of the seventh house I looked at that September day. It took a few minutes to recognize. I tapped my fingers on my steering wheel, looking at a plain, tiny, boring, white house with a big back yard, and I figured out the strange feeling when I said the words aloud, "This is mine. I belong here." For the first time in my life, I felt the security of homecoming.

When the real estate agent arrived, I bid on the house right there in the driveway.

"But, um, well, ma'am? You have found problems in every one of the first six houses we looked at. Don't you want to see the inside of this one?"

I smiled, not caring that I sounded like a lunatic. "Of course, I want to see the inside. After all, it is my home."

My little house was an instant haven and the security that I never knew I needed. There was no transition period necessary, and even the generally unsettling sounds of an old house settling were comfortable and familiar. I had been looking for a place where my son could put down roots, and discovered that, in this place, my own roots were waiting for me to arrive.

For almost a decade, my bond with home deepened. My son and I laughed, cried, loved, fought, prayed, played, worried, and learned. We adopted strays, both canine and human. In that house, I grew from the wandering girl who would walk away in an instant from people and places, without once looking back, to a woman with no need for a forwarding address.

Mother Nature had another plan.

Within a tragic timeframe of three days, over three hundred tornados hit the South. On the seventeenth anniversary of my little boy's birth, seven tornados touched down in our town. Despite the bad weather, my family held my son's birthday dinner at a restaurant across town. While we celebrated, an EF4 tornado visited my haven. By the time my child's birthday party ended, catastrophe had invaded our lives.

AT WORLD'S END

CHAPTER ONE

Mother Nature's Temper Tantrum

"Abandon hope, all ye who enter here."

-Dante Alighieri

It was only the wind that broke open the gates
between every day and never again. My memory of the resulting destruction that had once been my neighborhood is fractured, disjointed, and shocked. I write the narrative of the night my world ended in the manner I experienced it then, and how I have revisited it in countless nightmares. As I type this memory, that night is no longer in the past, again.

Telephone poles are flattened onto the torn ground. A labyrinth of power lines, seemingly benign, generates the possibility of electrocution. Fifty-year-old houses are smashed or missing. A pontoon boat performs a balancing act in the limbs of a twisted tree. Debris of ordinary lives produces mountains of confusion. I am lost in my own neighborhood, my internal guidance system disoriented by destruction.

"Jesus."

A Bronco reclines on a couch. Somebody has a couch that looks just like mine. Odd. Where am I? Shouldn't I be able to see my place from here? There are bits and pieces of property in the way; that cedar tree, ripped up by the roots, is blocking my view. Isn't that my tree? Someone is screaming further up the broken road. Screaming in horror. Screaming in pain. Then, silence.

"Oh, Jesus."

I climb across piles of wood and vinyl, shingles and concrete pieces, children's toys and furniture. I ascend cautiously, making certain that my weight will be held before I ask the devastation to hold it. I look closely before I set my handholds, in fear of slipping, of sliding down the jagged mountain, and of finding a neighbor's body. My hands scrape against broken glass and shingles. My high-heeled shoes slip and sink into itchy beds of pink insulation. Careful. Moving slowly, scanning the area at every step before I put my foot down, not looking for broken glass, but for victims. Careful. Power lines may be live, I can't tell. Don't touch them. Careful.

Standing on the unrecognizable remains of a house, this is some person's house. Climb down the other side. My right foot slips and lands on an afghan; black, white, orange and yellow- knitted by my grandmother's gifted hands. I bend down to touch it, thinking to pick it up, Mamaw's blanket, dirty on the ground. A single boot, the left boot of my most comfortable pair, lies inches from my trembling hand.

Imagining my house with broken windows. Blankets and shoes sucked out, but the rest intact. Frightened dogs hiding, behind the couch, maybe. I slowly turn to look back toward the Bronco, reclining on a…. and jerk to face forward again, popping a muscle in my neck. I hear myself murmur "Ouch" and raise my hand reflexively toward my neck, but the burning pain is distant. It should hurt but I do not quite feel it. My hand forgets its intent, wavers, and drops to my side. I am terribly confused. What was I just turning back to look at? Something bad. My mind, in self-defense, refuses to see it, refuses to let me turn around, and for a little while, it won't give me permission to remember. Trust instinct when the instinct says, very clearly, "No." Move forward, stepping over an afghan, lying tangled in the dirt. Careful.

"Oh, Jesus, please."

Keep going. My dogs. My dogs are in the house, terrified. I must get to them. I must move. Slow, careful, safe. They need me to get to them, soothe them. Panic, like a rat, begins chewing at my nerves, encouraging me to run, blindly. Home. Away. Anywhere. Just run. I take a breath, slowly enough to imagine that I am calm, and kick the panic-rat away. I know that panic, in this sharp and surreal landscape, will get me killed. My dogs need me to survive. They need me to rescue them. Cannot run. Damage can be fixed. Move ahead. Slowly. Carefully. Safely. Power line. Don't touch it. Go over or go under? Make a choice. This choice, in this moment, is all that exists. Over or under? Focus, girl!

"Oh, Jesus, please, Lord."

My cell phone rings, my ex-husband's number. When I had dropped my son off at his Dad's house, I had promised James that I would call when I got home. I answer and hear my almost grown, seventeen-year-old man-child say, "Mom? Mommy? Are you okay?"

I apply my best everything-is-just-fine-honey voice and tell him that the neighborhood is a bit of a mess, that I had to park on the corner and walk in, and I am not home just yet. I will call him back once I see "what's what". And, that I love him so much, so very, very much. I hang up the phone, take another slow breath, and move forward. Home. I just need to get home and all will be well. All is always well at home.

Belly crawl under power lines, through my neighbor's yard. A big tree crushes her roof. Chaos blocks the view of my own home. Look up at my neighbor standing, staring wide-eyed across the street toward my house. What do you see, woman? I dislike her expression when she looks down into my eyes. I dislike her apology-Why? Why is she sorry? I intensely dislike her poor grammar. "Gone" is a horrendous synonym for "damaged". I stand quickly, feel a power line brush my shoulder blades and freeze in terror of electrocution.

"Oh, Jesus, please, Lord God."

I am not electrocuted by my carelessness. I am not dead. I am in my neighbor's yard, in a place where I have stood many times over a decade. I see an empty space, only filled by the terrible night. Then, I see my own cute, little white home- picture window flanked by brown vinyl shutters, concrete stoop with the paint just starting to peel, dented screen door, scratched by the nearby bush. I see darkness. Home. Darkness. Faster and faster, flashing in my vision like strobe lights, I see what should be there, an entire house that my mind insists is still there, then the reality of gone. There. Gone. And, there, again. And, gone.

I close my eyes. Freezing water pours over my head, icy in three streaks on my scalp. Giant, dead fingers grip my head, squeezing the vision of home, flashing in and out of existence, trying to still it. The coldness drenches my body. There is no water, no fingers. My body reacts to the impending truth with shock, immersed in winter. My eyelids freeze shut and an icicle spears my heart. I force open my eyes, demanding that my brain allow my eyes to see what is really across the street. A woman, who sounds a little like me, speaks six words, quietly, woodenly, and not the hard, smooth, strong kind of building-wood, but the weather-beaten kind that splinters. I am not speaking. I am not feeling. I am seeing.

I see reality. It is nothing at all.

"Oh, Jesus, please, Lord God, no."

CHAPTER TWO

Hell's Evacuation

"Grief makes one hour ten."

– William Shakespeare

"Where were your dogs?" my neighbor asked.

"Inside…the house." I was so cold; it felt as if even my words were chunks of ice falling from my lips to break on the ground.

"Call them. Maybe they…maybe." She sobbed, but only once. They were not her dogs. "Call them."

I did. As loud as I could, in my best no-nonsense tone, I bellowed, "Captain Morgan! To ME!" A command.

"Shy! Mind me, now!"

The pair, identical mother and son, had been outside in their reinforced pen. The pen was gone, too, but maybe, maybe.

"Buddy!" I had crated my ancient wirehaired dachshund, before I left the house for dinner with the family. I had *crated* him, to keep him safe from the bigger dogs, in a house that had vaporized. "Bo-bos, Buddy, baby?" My voice cracked.

Louder. I howled into the empty night. "Chewy! Craaasssshhhh!" The twins, yin and yang in appearance and personality. Tears were burning hot tracks down my icy cheeks. My voice was already threatening to give out but I was not finished.

I roared, "GHOST!" and the volume of that name ripped something in my throat. I felt it tear. I felt it burn. I felt it break. I thought it might be my heart. I listened. Silence. Ghost was my special rescue dog, the one who responded to human emotions as if they were verbal commands. If Ghost could hear me, he would certainly answer me. My dogs were dead. I had no doubt. It crossed my mind, as my furry babies crossed to the other side, that they might still hear me and know I was there. I had not abandoned them. I was searching for them.

My breaking spirit needed their departed ones to know that. "BRUUU----UUCCCEE!" If grief were a word, it would sound like that one. I started coughing, and when I was done, I could not speak above a jagged whisper.

Everything I had known for a decade was entirely and absolutely gone, with no warning, not a result of any choice I had ever made. My world's random disappearance into oblivion had not required my presence. My spirit flickered for a moment, and then followed my beloved home into darkness.

Though what makes me, me, had crawled into some internal night, there were still things to do. When a reason for living is forgotten, sometimes instinct kicks in. Only two houses were still standing, and my neighbor and I hurried to check on the homebound occupants of the nearest one. The couple was alive, though severely shook up, and between us, we determined that most of our immediate neighbors had been away from home when the tornado hit.

Flashlights shone from up the hill. People from the subdivision were moving our way.

"We need to get out. There is another one coming!"

I remember speaking with my mother, stepmother, and sister-in-law on the phone. I still don't know if I called them or they called me. I shared the same information with each. My house was gone. Yes, I did mean gone. We were about to evacuate. I was unhurt and okay to drive. I would go to Mom's house. There was another tornado coming. Stay where they were. For God's sake, stay home and get in the basement. There was another one coming. I had to go, had to see to my neighbors.

Later, I discovered that not a single family member obeyed the "stay home" command.

I was angry because my most loved ones had put themselves in danger. "Mother! The last thing I said was that I could get out of the area and to stay put."

"No, the last thing you said was 'I have to go check on my neighbors'. If you had found someone injured, we all know that you would not have left him or her there. It wasn't that you could not get to safety. We just didn't know if you would."

My neighbor's son got my attention, and pointed to an animal peeking around a broken home, as I hung up the phone.

"Is that your dog?"

It was Captain Morgan. I called to him. He looked, wagged his tail once, and darted away, disappearing beneath the rubble. I went after him, tripping over debris, calling in my raspy voice, sure that he had not recognized me. He returned, and this time, Shy was with him. Captain had not run away when he saw me. He just went to fetch his mother. Another evacuee gave me his belt to use as a makeshift leash, but it was not necessary. The dogs stayed close.

A dozen evacuees huddled together, trying to discern a way out through the destruction. Some looked at the dark sky, as if they would catch the next round of tornados sneaking up on them. I looked, too. We quickly decided on an escape strategy. My neighbor, who had also walked in from where we parked at the corner gas station, would lead the way through the rubble's maze to relative safety. As she and I were the only two who entered from the direction the group now headed, I would leave last, following the evacuees, in case someone fell behind. There was no time for backtracking if anyone got lost.

There was little argument, no one in this group of strangers spoke much at all, and when anyone did, it was gently. Mostly, "Do you have a place to go? Do you have a way to get there? I do. Do you want to come with me?" Each individual focused on survival, and yet each stranger helped another through the catastrophe's labyrinth. When I noticed a couple with a baby following the group, I stopped, so they could catch up. The man fell, and the woman tried to help him up, with the baby still in her arms. I hurried back and we pulled the man to his feet.

What I remember about that night was the sensation of focus on our own survival. Aware only that another round of destruction prepared to rain down upon us, with no idea of when, and nowhere to hide, our situation was dangerous. Yet, once we helped the fallen man to his feet, I realized that the evacuation had paused. Each person, who was fleeing the area in order to survive, calmly waited on the stragglers to catch up though every wasted moment put lives at risk.

Before this terrible night, I equated the instinct for survival with selfishness. This example, in a group of strangers, showed me that we are not naturally solitary creatures. Humans are wired to require companionship, community, and connection. Biologically, we need a tribe, even a temporary, tornado-escaping one.

In the parking lot of the shattered, twisted structure that had formerly been the corner convenience store, I loaded my dogs into my car. I tried to call my son but my cell phone had no signal. Before I cranked the engine, I adjusted the rearview mirror to make sure Shy and Captain were settling into the backseat. In the mirror, I accidently caught sight of my own face. It was the color of a corpse. Even my lips were pale, and tears streamed down the lifeless cheeks. I had not even realized that I was still crying. As I looked into my own wide, unblinking, bloodshot eyes, my pupils appeared to be fixed. The panic-rat bit down, hard, and I slapped the mirror away. I did not even look like myself. I looked like a victim.

CHAPTER THREE

It's Always Darkest

"Nothing is inexorable but Love. Love which will yield to prayer is imperfect and poor."

–George MacDonald

The dreadful wind picked up as I drove away from my former neighborhood and I thought, "It's coming back for me." I remember the absolute terror, as the wind chased me along deserted streets, and still, I used my turn signals. That should not have been funny, but it was ridiculous. My laughter was scary, on the verge of hysteria, and I expected the next giggle to tip me over that edge.

I had previously warned everyone in my circle of friends and family that April 27 would be my last day as a smoker. I was quitting on April 28. The first thing I did, once I reached the relative safety of my brother's neighborhood, was stop at a convenience store to buy a pack of cigarettes. It was April 27, and it was 11:50 p.m.

I hesitated in the doorway of the convenience store, blinking at the painfully bright lights. It seemed that I had been in darkness for ages. I reached for my bag and did not have it. I remembered grabbing the backpack I used as a purse and deciding that I would only be away from home for a couple of hours. I would not need it, so I had tossed it on the couch. At least, I had shoved my ID and debit card in my back pocket.

I named my brand of smokes for the cashier, and she responded with the price. We were normal. I showed the cashier my ID, although she had not carded me, and I did not tell her that it was all I had left.

A few minutes later, I settled Captain and Shy on my brother's screened-in porch. I mass-texted my son and closest friends. My brother, Brian, asked why I was limping. I had no idea. I still don't know. His wife, Melody, looked

33

at my high-heeled shoes and filthy party clothes, and handed me tennis shoes and a change of clothes. They reassured me that my dogs would be fine, and I went to Mom's to spend the night.

Mom insisted that she slept better on the couch. I vaguely wanted to argue. I am naturally stubborn but argument had gone the way of everything I had ever known. Who I was, the part of me who insisted on allowing no one to sacrifice on my behalf, seemed so far beneath my surface, drowning. And, the part of me capable of swimming up through tragedy's depths long enough to respond to others, was already so weary. I obeyed quietly. I never asked her if my easy obedience unnerved her, as it did me. I did ask her, the next morning, if she had come into the bedroom while I slept. She had not even peeked in because she feared awakening me. That also unnerved me, because of my experience in that bedroom, but I did not tell her about it.

I sat on the end of my mother's bed, and pulled my knees to my chest. I balanced a pillow on my knees and buried my face in it, so my mother would not hear me sob. I prayed.

With every fiber of my soul and with every tear in my possession, I repeated a desperate plea.

"God, I have nothing to give you, except this unimaginable predicament. Devastation is not much of a gift, but it is all I have. You have to take responsibility for controlling this mess because I cannot even comprehend it. You control everything, even time, itself. You can undo this. You can take it all back. Tomorrow is in Your hands and You can make it so tonight is just a horrible nightmare. I believe, I believe. Thy will be done. Of course, thy will be done. But, Lord Jesus, if you love me... if you really love me, take it back. Take it back."

It was dark behind my eyelids, as lightless as my heart, soul, and mind. There seemed no light left in the world, and I felt that if I raised my head and opened my eyes, I would not be able to see. I put my feet on the floor, but continued to hold the pillow to my face, though it no longer mattered if my mother heard me cry. My mother, her couch, the next room, none of it existed. Only the darkness. It seemed that my despair had darkened the world, or I had gone blind. I realized the effect would be the same, and it did not matter. Nothing mattered. The unimaginable had not left me shattered. There were no pieces of me left, not that I could discern, only pain. I was a tiny void in the dark. I raised my head, eyes still closed, and the void cried out in a whisper.

"God, have mercy."

A light touch on my forehead and my mind exploded in white light, like an electrocution that I only felt in my brain. My eyes flew open, and I still could not see. I felt myself falling backwards, my feet still planted on the carpet, and the pillow falling out of my hand to the floor. Helplessly, as the back of my head touched the mattress, I thought one word- "aneurysm"- and then I was gone, swallowed by the darkness of deep sleep, in the last good night's rest I would have for a year.

I woke in the middle of the bed, my head on the pillow, with the blankets tucked completely around me, as I used to tuck in my son when he was small, "snug as a bug". My first thought was a disoriented, "This is not my bed." My second thought was a disorienting, "I will never wake up in my home, again."

The earliest morning sun lit the window. My prayer, "if you love me, take it back," had been answered. God had not unmade the disaster. God had said no. The day after the end of the world had begun and, against my wishes, I turned my face to that morning light.

CHAPTER FOUR

All the King's Horses and All the King's Men

"The darker the night, the brighter the stars,

The deeper the grief, the closer is God!"

-Fyodor Dostoevsky

I faced the dawn, sat up, and then slid out of bed to my knees on the floor. I bowed my head until it touched the carpet. No words materialized in my mind, and no emotion moved in my broken heart. My spirit had wailed itself empty the night before. I found no way to communicate from its depths. For the first time in my life, I felt too traumatized to pray. I knew God was still in His heaven but I could not sense my own soul in myself. I needed to pray, but my spirit was numb and silent.

Fear fluttered, its wings brushing my delicate core. I could not face this day without communicating with my God, my Lord, and my King. I decided to recite Scriptures and consider it as good as prayer. God would know that I was trying to reach Him. I searched my memory for any of the many verses I had pored over through the years. I realized that when I really needed a scripture, my disaster had torn away every Bible verse from my memory. Except one, Matthew 27:46, a pained accusation, a sincere question that many people have asked in the history of humanity. I did not want to insult God, and I certainly did not want Him to answer the question. But, it was the only thing I could think of to say to Him. My honesty in these words was as brutal as my circumstances. I hoped that my expected punishment, a result of my doubt, would be mild.

"My God, my God, why have you forsaken me?"

He began answering that question the instant I finished speaking, with a knock on the front door. A friend of my brother showed up with a brown paper bag full of clothing in approximately my size. God continued repeating His answer, countless times, in various ways, through different people, during the course of that day. I'm sure that not an hour passed that God failed to repeat the answer to that question.

I asked Him, once, "My God, why have you forsaken me?"

He repeated His reply often, in that nasty, horrible, no-good, very bad day, and in the harder months to come, "My child, I haven't."

After showering, I dressed in someone else's clothes and dried my hair. I looked in the mirror, noting that I felt rested but looked tired. Then, I leaned closer to the mirror, running my fingers through my hair. Was it possible that I was just noticing this?

"Mom!" I bellowed. "Mom, come and look at my hair!" I did not wait for her to answer. I ran to the living room and knelt before her in the light from her lamp, still tugging at my mud-brown mane, while part of my mind informed me that freaking out over my hair was silly. My house was destroyed, my dogs were dead, and I was obsessing over my hair.

My mother inspected my hair with little interest. She knew I had bigger problems. "You mean the gray streaks?"

"Um, yeah! You saw me yesterday."

"I was upset last night."

"Okay, I'll give you that. I was, too. But, I came over yesterday afternoon. Did my hair…, look at me, Mom…, have these two big gray streaks?"

"Three." She corrected calmly, "There is one on top." She firmly stroked each streak, and my body went cold, remembering the icy, giant fingers gripping those three exact spots the night before when I saw that my house was missing. I shuddered and pulled away.

"And, no. Your hair was not gray yesterday."

"And you don't think this is weird?"

She shrugged. "You have had a shock and your hair turned gray. It happens."

"No, it doesn't. That is a myth. It's impossible."

She gave me a withering look. "Go look in the mirror again. Obviously, it does happen."

I did just that.

Half an hour after the discovery that I had gone gray overnight, I purchased dog food for my two survivors, relocated during the aftermath to my brother's porch. When I handed the smallest bag of dog food I have purchased in years to the cashier, he asked, "How are you today?" I smiled brightly and lied, "Just fine!" As he scanned the little bag, it crossed my mind that I only had two dogs left to feed, because the others must have been killed.

I handed the cashier my debit card, while tears rolled down my cheeks. I did not expect to cry. I had noted no warning signs. I did not sniffle. I did not gasp. I did not sob. Just a thought and then those silent tears, pouring two tiny waterfalls onto the cashier's counter. The boy looked shocked when he glanced at my face and opened his mouth to speak. I shook my head, and he closed it again, handing over my debit card with wide eyes. Nothing, not the pride I take in my self-control, not my disdain for public scenes, nor the knowledge that I did not even possess a Kleenex, could stop those tears. I could not even bring myself to wipe the humiliating sorrow away with my hand. I was helpless, I was powerless, and several people were staring at me.

A hand landed gently on my shoulder, warm and comforting. The strange woman said nothing. Neither did I. She squeezed my shoulder for about a minute, as a peace that passes all understanding filled me. By the time she released me, my sudden tears had ceased. She wore overalls. She had direct, kind green eyes. That is all I know about this woman. She was just an ordinary person who may never know how the instinctive, compassionate touch of her hand soothed the ruptured heart of a grieving tornado victim. I tried to smile, failed, settled for a nod, and left the store carrying a little bag of dog food and the strength I had borrowed from a stranger's love.

In the parking lot, my phone rang. My friend did not even say hello. She asked, "What do you need?"

"I really don't know. I'm running errands now, so the roads will be clear before I go...," I swallowed, "...home. I'll know more when I see that mess in daylight."

"Then, you need breakfast." An order. I never ate breakfast. But, I met her where she told me to meet her, and I ate what I was served.

At breakfast, she introduced me to her friend and they decided that I needed shopping for essentials. They also decided that I did not need to pay for those items. I have always been independent, stubborn about doing things my way, making my own decisions, and never accepting charity. It seemed that disaster had wiped out even my personality characteristics.

My boss called, as my friends were piling new clothes into my unresisting arms. "Our co-workers went to your... your place with chainsaws to help clear, um, debris. They think they spotted one of your dogs. They said they can't catch it."

Catch it? That implied…The purchases fell out of my hands.
"Alive?"

I raced out of the store, calling an explanation over my
shoulder to my friends. It is a good thing that I dropped my
purchases because I would have inadvertently shoplifted, at
top speed, while dodging shopping carts, customers, and
small children. Speeding home, I discovered my ability to
pray had returned. Simultaneously, I thanked and begged
God for my dog, any of my dogs. I asked Him to brace me
for disappointment, as it might not even be my dog. I cried
in fear and for my loss of the others while rejoicing for the
unidentified survivor, too.

Closer to my neighborhood, traffic suddenly increased and I
did not understand why. As my car crept impatiently along,
I looked at the effects of the previous night's bedlam. It
looked even worse in daylight. I talked to myself, repeating
the same command until I reached the driveway to a
nowhere that had been my home.

"Be brave. Be brave."

My co-workers had not spotted one of my dogs, but four of them. When I leapt out of my car, Kevin was speaking urgently into his phone. Greg cradled my little Buddy who was lying very still. I tried to stick my car keys in my pocket, realized that I was wearing someone else's pants and they did not have pockets, and just threw my keys on the ground on the way to grab my littlest dog. I said Buddy's name and only knew he was alive when he lifted his head at the sound of my voice. He was miraculously uninjured. Dee had dug Buddy out of a muddy hill, leaving a deep dachshund imprint behind in the dirt. Several days later, I dug Buddy's crate out from under rubble. It was crushed, but the door was still latched.

Chewy heard my voice when I arrived. I saw her white head pop up above the brush, black ears lifted, and then I only saw a quick white blur until the little hound launched herself into my arms. Dee described a black and white boxer mix that had resisted her rescue attempts and escaped. That was my Crash.

Then Dee told me to remain calm because Kevin was already calling a veterinarian, but they had just found an injured dog, an old German Shepherd/Collie mix, trapped beneath a downed tree. A sheet of plywood hid him from view. When I tossed the plywood aside, I could see the white bones and red tendons of his mangled front leg, the agony in his eyes, and the familiar doggy-smile of my beloved Ghost Li. He licked my hand, swishing his tail. I asked him to be brave, and Ghost did his best to be A Good Boy while we broke branches, lifted the tree, and, carefully, slid his wounded body out. We used the plywood as a stretcher and loaded my dog into the back of Greg's truck. I joined him, uncaring where we were going, as I buried my face in Ghost Li's fur and repeated "Good Boy. It will be okay. Lie still. Best Boy." Kevin followed in my car, with Chewy in the backseat. Buddy stayed with Dee.

When we arrived at the vet's office, Greg leaned against the truck, waiting for the veterinary technicians to bring a stretcher for Ghost. "Don't worry about paying for this. Our co-workers want to help you, so we already arranged for all of them to donate to Ghost's care. Sweetie, don't cry."

More surprise tears. I was doing it, again.

I wanted to stay with my dog, but I had so many other pressing things to deal with, too. Chewy waited in my car. Responsibility trumped feelings, and I consoled myself with the fact that Ghost Li would be unconscious. He would not even know I was gone.

I saw my Ghost into surgery, which would take several hours and possibly end in amputation, then returned home. My son had arrived and I tried to comfort him, even as he tried to comfort me.

As I knelt on the foundation of my home, I looked around and tried to come up with a strategy. Across the street, I could see several untidy piles containing different rooms of my house. I saw a Bronco parked on my couch, and remembered what my mind had forced me to deny knowing the night before. Blocks away, pieces of my life scattered. It was just stuff, but it was also more than that. Each item packed with a beloved memory was broken. All that was familiar was devastated. My past had led me to my home, and my future began there. The starting point, the foundation, the anchor from which I had begun each project and every dream was a ruin. I had never experienced a mess of this magnitude, and it was my mess to clean up. Where would I start? What could I do? It was just too big for me. I prayed one word. Help.

I heard my name shouted several times, and regained my feet as a small crowd of people jogged over the hill, co-workers, school friends, church friends, all those who heard about the disaster and, coincidentally, showed up at the same time, in the moment I needed someone most. One was actually wearing pajamas and slippers. I raised my hand and waved.

I recognized the group for what it was. The cavalry had arrived. I stepped into the road, opened my arms wide, and waited for my running friends to surround and support me.

CHAPTER FIVE

Port-A-Potty Princess

"I know not all that may be coming, but be it what it will, I'll go to it laughing."

-Herman Melville

My child was a seventeen-year-old boy on the night that Mister Twister invaded. I watched him handle the destruction of our lives with a wicked humor, and work in the rubble of our home with innate responsibility. My little boy looked different to me. When I suddenly recognized that difference, my heart overflowed with both intense pride and maternal sorrow.

Overnight, James had become a seventeen-year-and-one-day-old man. He had been a good boy one day, and the next day, he was a wonderful man.

As sweat poured down his face, he held on to his gorgeous smile, joking through his own pain while he trashed his prized possessions, offering water and reminding volunteers to stay hydrated, helping neighbors haul debris, and regularly giving his old mother a smile, a hug or a quick hand-squeeze. Truly blessed, I had given birth to my own hero. I could charge Hell, itself, armed only with a bucket of water, as long as my son was at my side.

The afternoon after the end, my son got his first glimpse of the tornado's horrific handiwork. He greeted me with a hug, and then said, "Mom, you said you were going to quit smoking!" I looked at the cigarette between my fingers, a little shamefully.

"I know."

"Remember, you told me that you wouldn't quit until after my birthday. You said that the day after my birthday, you were going cold turkey and all hell would break loose around here."

"I remember." I replied, as my son took a good, long look around at the rubble of our life, gestured at the hell that had actually broken loose, and gave me his I'm-such-a-funny-guy grin.

"Look at this mess. Why didn't you just light up?"

I laughed, hard and genuine, chasing away a little of the mind-numbing fog that catastrophe had delivered.

Mister Twister had scattered our house, a panorama of destruction. As I carefully picked my way through the new terrain, I tried to orient myself, to make sense of the mess.

I pointed to an empty metal tub in the center of my empty foundation. "What is that?" A high school buddy looked inside.

"It's the tub to a washing machine. There are clothes still in here." He pulled out a handful of articles of clothing. Mud dripped from them. "These are filthy. I think your washer is defective."

"Oh, just run it through another cycle." I grinned and felt a little bit more human.

A single kitchen chair looked lonely in my backyard. The rest of the house had blown across the street. I walked about a quarter of a mile, identifying pieces of my property, before giving up the search and turning back. I walked around a refrigerator in the street. It was not mine. I never found my kitchen. When I mentioned it, someone suggested putting up flyers.

My son's basketball goal lay across part of his bedroom wall. The mountain of wreckage I had scaled the night before appeared to be my living room, mostly.

The bottom half of my dresser sat near a ditch, one drawer open. I removed a roofing shingle, and peeked inside. The pajamas inside were neatly folded. My bras and underwear had been in the top half of the dresser. Too bad. I would have liked to wear my own panties for a change. I shrugged, a little surprised that I had the capacity to shrug at all this, and moved on.

As I climbed over a pile of ruins about four feet high, I recognized the intact floor's linoleum pattern.

"Hey, I found the bathroom!" I exclaimed, and balanced on my floor, which, in turn, balanced on top of a pile of unrecognizable disarray. I looked around, wondering where the rest of the loo had gone.

My ex-husband approached and spoke to me. As I looked down to reply, I saw James stomp toward us, glaring at his Dad.

"Dad! Show some respect. Don't talk to my mom right now. Can't you see she is in the bathroom?"

His father snapped back, "Well, she didn't bother to close the door."

I laughed so hard that I almost fell off the bathroom.

With the help of volunteers, we carried our debris back to our property, sorted, and inventoried it. In our front yard,

James sat down in my recliner, which was broken and leaning to the right, in front of our television with the giant hole in the screen.

"Mom! I want to watch a different show. Have you seen the remote?" He grinned.

"No. Have you checked under the couch cushions?" I called back.

"Not yet. Where is the couch?"

"It's under the neighbor's car, honey. But, the batteries might be dead."

A sigh. "Oh, I'll just watch this show, I guess."

We laughed. Our family and friends laughed. The neighbors laughed. Volunteers stared at us, afraid to laugh, as we combated disaster by the strategic use of silliness.

We joked in the face of our pain, and mocked our own tragedy because we knew, instinctively, that if you can laugh at something, then you can survive it.

"Sorry, the house is such a mess. It is the maid's day off."

James found a light switch and flicked it. "Guys, the power is out. Did someone forget to pay the utility bill?"

A co-worker arrived as I was sitting on my back steps, which led to nowhere, now, and sorting through my ruined books. "What can I do to help? Whatever you need me to do, I'll do."

"You get the hard job." I handed her a bent broom. "Here. Sweep the kitchen for me."

She took the broom, confused, and slowly looked around, "Um, okay? Where's your kitchen?"

I managed to keep a straight face. "That's why it's the hard job. You have to find it, first."

If I had not been a disaster victim, she might have hit me with the broom.

The Red Cross drove through and asked what we needed. Tarps? Bottled water? Sandwiches? I responded, "A place to pee would be fantastic, if you happen to have one on hand." Within thirty minutes, they delivered a port-a-potty to my front yard. It was decidedly convenient, and a source of great amusement. With the only working toilet in the neighborhood, we joked about being "the classy family", and mentioned raising funds by charging admission.

A friend approached me in the middle of the rubble, and whispered in my ear.

"Should I look for anything special?"

Special? What was she talking about? "If you find anything unbroken, it will be special." I sighed.

"I mean, um, maybe from your bedroom?" She gave me an intent look, willing me to know what she was implying.

I didn't. "My bed? My bed is still missing. Why are we whispering?"

"Something special. From your bedroom. Maybe you kept one in your underwear drawer?"

Why on earth was she still whispering? My underwear scattered all over the neighborhood. Everyone had already seen it. She could mention my delicates out loud. At this point, modesty was a farce. I just gave her a blank look.

She spoke slowly, carefully emphasizing certain words. "Did you own anything *special*? A *secret* thing that some *single* women own? Something that *hums*?"

Oh. Oh! Oh, no! I was so shocked by the question that I forgot to whisper. "No! I did not ever own one of those secret somethings! If you find anything that hums, it certainly is not mine!"

She covered her face. I blushed. Nearby victims and volunteers laughed.

Over the next several days, the neighborhood continued sorting our broken possessions, helping each other with the community mess. My best friend picked up a sweater and held it in the air. "Becca, is this yours?" She held it to her ear. "Oh, it must be yours. It doesn't hum!"

A neighbor held up a lamp. "This must be Rebecca's lamp. It isn't humming."

My son's smiling friend walked past me several times. He was humming a tune. He obviously wanted me to ask. "What are you doing?"

"Making sure people don't mistake me for your son."

We laughed. All of us laughed, a lot. We could survive this catastrophe, but not without laughter. The hilarity was never forced, but sprang from the simple, miraculous fact that we lived. Humor was as much a natural part of our existence as tragedy had become.

With a teenage volunteer, I spent several minutes trying to figure out what the black piece of metal wrapped around, and embedded in, my downed pine tree was. I finally figured it out when I made out part of the brand name. "It's my microwave."

We looked at each other and the boy uttered a common descriptive phrase, always applicable to the effects of that terrible wind. We used it, often.

"Just wow, man."

As we returned to our work, the teenager absently hummed a tune I knew. I sighed and stared at him until I realized that he was not humming as a joke. The kid was just humming. He recognized the offensiveness of that song under these circumstances, and looked at me, horrified. At the same moment, I recognized how perfect the chorus was for these circumstances. I began singing, and he joined in, relieved. Neither of us was absolutely sure of all the lyrics, so we giggled and improvised. When we got to the chorus, we owned that part, our singing loud and heartfelt, if not harmonious. It became a song my own son and I sang often. It just fit.

It really was the end of the world, as I knew it. But, I felt fine.

CHAPTER SIX

Promised Land

"One must still have chaos in oneself to be able to give birth to a dancing star."

–Friedrich Nietzsche

During the weeks of cleaning up the shattered remains of my ended life, I noticed each painful moment as I trashed every little thing. I reminded those who seemed almost horrified at my cold treatment toward my possessions that "It's just stuff." Yet, I squeezed each item, ever so briefly, and dug a little grave for the attached memory in the aching tissue of my heart. The vast wave of of empathy from so many people crushed me beneath the weight of the awe it inspired. I looked closely at every broken object and saw it as it had once been, when the possession was an unnoticed piece of my every day, safe life. Then, I named it "just stuff" and threw it away.

My days consisted of backbreaking work at "the site". I consumed my evenings by sorting through garbage bags full of my writings and my son's grade school drawings, futilely hoping for anything salvageable. Fiberglass insulation embedded in each page and I wore protective gloves, saddened by the thought that I could not touch my baby's artwork with my bare hands. Each long night, I stared at my mother's ceiling until physical exhaustion dragged me into nightmares.

An inescapable, unanswerable question echoed, regardless of what I was actually doing. My friends asked. My family asked. Strangers asked. Every step I would take hinged on the right decision, and I had no idea what that answer was. I prayed repeatedly, and God was silent.

What am I going to do, now?

Almost everyone who loved me had an opinion. People who did not even know me had an opinion. Those who did not have an opinion, awaited mine, wanting to help. The choice to sell my land, move somewhere else, and start a brand new thirty-year mortgage was the majority vote. The reasons for moving on were many and quite logical. With a tiny insurance policy, few resources, and no experience, rebuilding was impossible, and still I considered it.

I considered options carefully, and logically, while my heart childishly cried out, "I want to go home."

I knew what I wanted. What I wanted was insanity to even consider, but was it the right call? I prayed and prayed. However, God did not speak. I felt His presence every moment, in the peace that surpassed my understanding and in the agony that surpassed mere emotion. Only He could show me His way, and He was not talking.

I waited until my mother left for work. I placed a Bible on the couch and knelt before the unopened book. Then, audaciously, I called God out.

"I know what I want. You know what I want. I want to go home. But, we don't need to talk about what I want, because

I don't need what I want. I need what You want for me, only that. I will do anything You say, even if it's hard. But, You have to tell me. Now. Thy will be done. But I need to know what Your will is."

I made my puny threat, to show God that I meant business. "I am on my knees before You, Father. I will not get up from this spot until You answer me clearly, no matter what the answer is. I will not eat, I will not drink, I will not move. I will pray until You answer me. I will wet my pants if you make me wait long enough, and then I will tell my mother to blame You for the urine stain on her carpet. I mean it, God; I must know what You want me to do. All in your time, Lord, but I am kneeling right here and I am waiting for your time. Speak Thy damn will!"

I waited for a moment, and continued. "I am not asking for a map, Lord. I am not requesting a blueprint. I do not need detailed directions, not yet. We can work that out as we go. I am begging for just one word. My choice is give up, sell out, run away from all of this pain, and buy some random house, or stay and fight and go home to my land.

It is a simple question, Father.

House or land?

Give me a simple answer.

One word is all I ask.

One or the other, Your choice.

House or land?

Please.

I prayed there for hours, until my knees ached, and my back throbbed. I was thirsty and I felt a sincere and painful desire to go to the bathroom. There was no still small voice, no sensation of being led in any direction. Yet, I had committed to pray through, patiently. I am not a patient person. God knows this.

This is the point in the story where a good Christian girl would open the Bible lying on the couch. However, this is my story, instead. And, I am not a very good girl. I did not open that Bible. I smacked it, crying "God, c'mon! Answer me. It's easy. Everybody says buy a house, give up, and run away. Do I do that? Or, do I fight them all to live on my land? I am doing nothing, here. What do You want me to do? What do You say? House or land?"

The holy book fell on the floor, open, and I stretched so I could reach where it landed without leaving my knees. I already knew I should not have hit the Bible, and there is probably some Scripture written in it about not slapping God's Word around. Guiltily, I pulled the book toward me. I looked at the open pages, planning to read since God obviously wasn't listening to my prayers right now, anyway. At first glance, I read two verses.

"[So they said] Arise, let us go up against them. For we have seen the land and, indeed, it is very good. Would you do nothing? Do not hesitate to go, that you may enter to possess the land.

When you go, you will come to a secure people and a large land. For God has given it into your hands, a place where there is no lack of anything that is upon the earth." –Judges 18: 9 & 10

The word "land" repeated three times. The word "house", not mentioned once. Direction. In addition, a bonus gift, a promise from my Father. Arise; let US go up against them. I would not fight alone.

The coming months would be a fight against those who loved, pitied, and demanded what was "best" for me. The next year would contain a series of epic battles against the emotional and psychological damage that Mother Nature had inflicted on me. I would struggle painfully against both doubt and faith. I would spend hours in prayer, decorating a tomb for the person I still wanted to be. Forever changed, I would argue with God over choosing the person I must become. God had told me where I would end up, and I was grateful, determined to hold onto that promise. Later, I would wish I had also asked the questions "How?" and "When?" But the truth is that I did not need to know, not then.

This knowledge of an impending personal war for my home and my sanity, a war I was ill equipped to enter, terrified me. Awareness tempered my vulnerability. I would not go into these battles unarmed.

My weapon was faith, and if I refused to let it fall from my hands, or if it did fall, and I just picked it right back up, then I, also, held a hope within my hurt.

My Father had promised.

I was going home.

First, I gently closed my Bible and sincerely gave thanks. Then, I hurriedly went to the bathroom. After that, I grabbed a yellow legal pad that I had been using as a to-do list, and titled it "Project Normalcy". It would eventually fill both sides of thirty-four pages, and become a dirty, tattered, tear-stained map of my road home.

THE LIMBO

CHRONICLES

CHAPTER SEVEN

Hope and Cockroaches

"Accept whatever comes to you woven in the pattern of your destiny, for what could more aptly fit your needs?"

–Marcus Aurelius

The storm had reduced my haven to a broken foundation, stolen a lifetime worth of possessions filled with beloved memories, and destroyed those landmarks that made my place recognizable. My little family was ripped to its individual components. My son stayed at his father's house. I slept on my mother's couch. My surviving dogs went to separate foster homes and boarding kennels.

71

I needed all of us to be together again. The story of my life, as I knew it, had ended, but there must be a sequel. I watched my teenage son handle the catastrophe with humor, dignity, and responsibility, transitioning in a single, terrible night from a boy to a man. With this amazing guy at my left hand, and my God at my right, we could begin again. Beneath the Really Big Mess, my land waited for my family's return. But more than anything, even more than home, my family required each other.

I rented temporary headquarters, a rest stop for my son, one dog, per the rental contract, and myself, in a cheap trailer park. It did not take long to move in, because we did not own anything, anymore. The ceiling leaked, it was stifling without air conditioning, and the present tenants, a disgusting family of cockroaches, fought the eviction. I unhappily shared the tiny shower with water bugs. My human neighbors dwelled mere yards away, when I was accustomed to an acre of personal space.

Choosing only one dog to live with us was a difficult, yet simple decision. Both Chewy and Buddy were doing well with their respective foster families. Shy and Captain were together. The trailer had steps, and Ghost Li could not handle steps during the months of his recovery and rehabilitation from his injuries. He was safe and happy with my best friend's family. Crash was not doing well, at all.

Over a week after the storm, I had found Crash cowering under a bush, not far from our former home. When he saw me, his eyes widened, his body stiffened and his ears went back. I knew that after a natural disaster, smells in the area change, and often, terrified pets cannot find their way home due to this. I waited, talking softly. He was just scared and did not recognize me yet. I wondered if my own scent had changed. Recognition would only take a moment, surely. After all, I had nursed Crash, due to many accidental injuries, through most of his puppyhood and he was quite attached to me.

His face looked funny. I could see his teeth, and I stepped forward, trying to see him better. Had he suffered a facial injury? It looked deformed, somehow. I heard a sound that I had never heard from any of my own dogs, and the volume increased when I leaned closer. It actually took me a minute to recognize the sound and realize why my dog's face looked odd.

My own dog was snarling at me. My feelings were hurt, as I stepped back. A fellow animal-rescuer stood several yards away from us, and called to me softly. "Do you need me to get a muzzle from my car?"

A muzzle.

For Crash?

I did not want to muzzle my sweet dog. My sweet dog was growling at me.

Reality is more important than feelings. You do what you've got to do.

"Yes," I spoke softly, as well. "And a pair of bite gloves, if you have them."

She hurried away and I squatted down, in a nonthreatening manner. I kept talking to Crash, avoiding direct eye contact with him. His growls diminished. Out of the corner of my eye, I saw his head cock to one side and I looked directly at him. He looked back at me, and in that moment, he actually saw me for the first time. His eyes widened, his ears lifted and the tip of his tail wagged, slowly, hopefully. He stretched his neck, stuck only his nose out of the bushes, and sniffed, hard. Very hard.

I whispered, "Do you know me, now?"

He launched himself at my face. I instinctively blocked my throat, but felt no teeth, only lots of puppy-tongue.

My friend hurried back, as Crash joyfully leaped five feet in the air over and over, licking my face at every bounce while I laughed.

"Don't need the muzzle, now?"

"Nope!" I caught my dog mid-leap and hugged him, then released the ecstatic mutt.

"Leash?"

"Do you think I need one?"

"Nope!"

Crash was my sweet, loving dog, again, but he now refused to allow strangers near him. He growled and snapped and I could not send him to any foster home. It wasn't safe. Instead, he stayed at a fancy boarding kennel, where he had the best food, shelter, his own little cot, and the solitary confinement he needed. No one touched him. He was miserable.

Crash needed to be with me, in order to be himself again.

The temporary trailer allowed my dog to be with those he loved best. My family was united, at least, partially. It was cheap. In addition, my beloved former sister-in-law's family lived in the trailer park. As donated furniture and other belongings trickled in, as I pored over homeowner's insurance paperwork, and as I arranged our existence, sandwiched between past and future, I felt both agonized and blessed.

I began to realize that loss and gratitude are never separate, but linked. Hope and doubt can co-exist, as can fear and faith. Joy exists in sorrow, not despite it. Miracles are not located at the end of suffering, but within it. I was convinced that God would send me home. I decided that I must be strong enough to handle the physical labor, smart enough to perform the mental gymnastics, faithful enough to face the spiritual challenges, and brave enough to overcome the psychological damage. If I could pass these tests, then home would be the prize. Until then, this bug-infested, leaky tin can was exactly where I needed to be.

I refused to refer to the trailer as "home". I had a Home, in past and in future, and that tin can certainly was not it, no matter how long we would be forced to inhabit it. My son suggested that we give the trailer a name. He understood why I could not bear to use the word 'home' but 'the-place-we-are-temporarily-staying-until-we-can-rebuild-and-go-to-our-real-home-again' was a bit of a mouthful.

"Well, we are in between our own personal hell, and home", I joked. "The place between heaven and hell is generally called Limbo." We named both the tin can dwelling, and that phase of our lives, Limbo.

CHAPTER EIGHT

Tornado Chick

"Father, forgive them, for they do not know what they do." –Jesus Christ (Luke 23:34)

Some people make the front page of the local newspaper because they do something important, or because something important is done to them. I ended up in an edition of the local newspaper because someone took the newspaper that belonged to me.

As any other ordinary mother, I saved the newspaper from the day my little boy was born. The headline on that memorable day in 1994 was "Killer Tornado Strikes Indiana Town" and some of the disaster volunteers found that coincidence interesting. I was just happy to have a little piece of my past, intact. The newspaper wandered around my neighborhood, passed from hand to hand, while I went back to work, salvaging damage. It disappeared at some point.

Later, a local reporter left a message. She wanted to interview me about the tornado and my newspaper. My initial response was to deny the request, as I am a very private person and the reporter could choose from a plethora of victims. However, a friend called, who was helping me look for Bruce. As she had formerly worked in media, I mentioned the reporter's call, and she advised that I do the interview and request that my missing dog be mentioned in the article.

I decided that, though I hated the idea of being in the local spotlight, even for a day, and despised the thought of my business aired publically, I could put up with the personal discomfort in order to get more people looking for my Bruce. I assumed that people who knew me would make a bigger deal over the interview than it really was. I could handle that, to find Bruce. A neighbor had seen him the day after the tornado, but there was no sign of him since. I checked the animal shelter daily, my friends and family walked the blasted neighborhoods, and I had even called in my former boyfriend to help with the search.

I arranged to meet with the reporter at the site of my former home, not to display my loss, but because I had work to do there. I do not know how to be interviewed, so we just chatted, while I transferred brand names and serial numbers from my broken appliances to the property lists. She asked how I was feeling, and I responded, "Blessed." She looked at me in disbelief. "Seriously. I am alive. My son is alive. A lot of people..." I gestured to my destroyed neighborhood, "are in this boat, with me. People died. People do not have insurance. People do not have families to stay with. I do. I am blessed, more than I deserve to be. Most of my house blew away from my property. As far as clean-up goes, I have it easier than a lot of people. I just want to finish cleaning up my mess and go help with theirs. "

She asked about the newspaper, and I admitted that I had saved it, along with most of my son's childhood drawings and schoolwork. She looked sad, at that. "Look," I said quickly, "I lost that stuff. I lost the baby book. I lost the baby's artwork. And, I still have the baby. I still have my son. Everything else is just stuff. We have our lives and we have our foundation." I patted the broken chunk of concrete I sat upon, in a friendly manner. "We can build on this." I did not want to talk about all I had lost. I did not want to be a victim. So, I steered the conversation to what remained.

I told her about my former husband showing up to help. My ex hated me at one time and vice versa, until we learned to be civil over the years of parenting a most beloved child, and finally developed an acquaintanceship. My former husband became a genuine friend in a moment, surrounded by the rubble of my life, when I learned that my neighbor had asked him if we were finding any property that could be saved. My ex answered, "I'm not looking for stuff to salvage. I am just searching for her photographs of our son. That is what she will miss most so I'm trying to find some of them."

We talked about looters, and agreed that a person had to be a real piece of garbage to steal from those who had already had so much stolen by Mother Nature. My stuff had been stolen, but the patrolling police officers had caught a couple of the thieves in the act, tracked down their comrades and some of my stuff, and returned it, before I even noticed that my belongings had been stolen, instead of just moved during clean-up. I laughed and said, "I wonder if the cop who brought my stuff back knew how dangerously close he came to receiving a kiss from a skinny, filthy, homeless woman?"

I was as grateful that the police kept traffic moving through the neighborhood and attempted to reroute the asinine people who just drove through to gawk.

I added that the rubberneckers, or sightseers, were as bad as the looters, or worse. "Thieves know that they are thieves. Sightseers think their hurtful behavior is acceptable."

The reporter asked about the town's response to our crisis. "They really stepped up. And, that really, really surprised me. This is a Bible-belt town, and I have never seen it act in a Christian manner, before this. It's too bad that a disaster has to occur for people to behave like humans, but, at the same time, there is hope in it."

The conversation turned to Bruce. "Bruce is my last irreplaceable. Everyone else is accounted for. When I find him, my family will be complete. That is the only reason I am talking with you, honestly. I need to find my dog, and I need help."

She asked if I wanted to let the community know anything else. "No. Wait. Yes. Yes, there is." The reporter waited while I gathered my thoughts, trying to find a way to express them. "Can you tell the sightseers, the people driving around taking pictures for the fun of it, to stop? Someone might get hurt. Specifically, I might hurt someone. Maybe they don't realize it, how mean it is. They drive by, they take pictures, and we can hear them talking about how "cool" it all is, "like a movie", and it isn't.

"It is our lives and our pain that entertain the sightseers. They enjoy this, and then, they get to go home. That is the one thing that no disaster victim is allowed right now, to go home, to be normal. Not right now, and maybe, not ever again. It is similar to people rubbernecking at a car wreck. Someone's life has changed, drastically, and there is no compassion. It is self-absorbed behavior, it is bad manners, and it is cruel. Someday, I will try to forgive them, but please, ask them to never do it, again."

She asked permission to take a couple of photographs. I rolled my eyes and smiled, "As long as you don't ask me to like it. I assumed that pictures would be part of the deal." Later, as she packed away her notebook and camera, she commented on my positive attitude. "I'm not an annoying little Positive Polly, you know. I am a realist and I try to be fair. A terrible thing happened here. But, honey, look around. Those people over there, dropping off cases of water, and those people with the chainsaws, helping clear debris, and those teenagers, who have been here before eight o'clock in the morning every single day? Most of those people are strangers, and all of them are good.

If you look for the good in all of this terrible, you will see it. There is certainly suffering here. The blessings deserve equal time and attention. They are not as obvious, but they are just as real."

The article printed, and as promised, the search for Bruce was mentioned. Suddenly, everyone knew me.

I had expected family, friends, and acquaintances to mention the front-page article, to bring copies, as if I cared, but they would understand that this piece of paper was nothing of importance to me. I had not had time to watch the news or read a newspaper. In fact, I had not seen a single bit of coverage about the tornados. My family was too busy dealing with the aftermath to watch it or read about it. It never crossed my mind that others would.

Suddenly, cashiers, waitresses, people at the animal shelter, and random shoppers in stores recognized my face, and they all wanted to talk to me about my least favorite subject. Of course, not every person wanted to discuss my personal tragedy, but many did. As a natural introvert whose nerves were already raw, it caused quite a bit of anxiety. I never got used to, "You look familiar. Oh, I read about you in the paper! You are the tornado chick!" All I wanted was to buy toilet paper, like a normal person, and the cashier wanted to tell all her tornado stories to a victim, to Tornado Chick.

When a woman I had never met struck a sympathetic tone in a grocery store line, I knew that no subject was off limits when aimed at Tornado Chick.

"Oh, honey, this must be such a terrible time for you, especially now, as I see you are buying pads. You know that stress brings on a heavier flow. You should put those generic ones back and get something more suitable for you." Even my menstrual cycle and my choice in feminine hygiene products were suddenly available for public discussion.

My entire life was reduced to a pile of rubble, my private tragedy available for public consumption, and my identity reduced to a single event, the worst event of my life.

Strangers knew what I looked like. They knew where I had once lived, where I spent most of my time. Some wanted to help, out of the kindness of their hearts, and others wanted to help because I was "famous".

Christians and atheists, alike, had raced to my aid. Christians both prayed and acted, simultaneously. The Religious Folk, on the other hand, gave me a "good talking to". It was pretty easy to tell the difference between Christian and Religious, whether the person who approached me was a friend, acquaintance or just a newspaper-reading complete stranger.

"I prayed so hard for my own loved ones that night. I bet you wish someone had prayed for you."

What makes you think no one did?

"God punishes sin with natural disasters."

Seven tornados destroyed countless small town lives in one day. You better get started officially changing the name of this town to Gomorrah.

"Why didn't you have a husband to protect you, anyway?"

Because I did not realize that "outdoor plumbing" would fend off a natural disaster. How would that work, exactly?

"God did this to you. You were living in sin with a man, for a while. You deserved this."

I deserved none of this, not the suffering, and not the kindnesses that followed. Period.

"God did not protect you."

I am alive.

"God does not love you."

Liar.

I refrained from punching any of them in the face. I pasted on a polite smile and I practiced being a lady.

Christians supported my faith when it wavered. As for the Religious Folk, when they insist on creating doubt in God's love for their neighbor, I believe they sin. I hope they get to answer to my God for that and not their own god, because their god is a big meany.

Hard questions during tough times are always acceptable. I never expected the number of people who dropped those tough, heartfelt questions at my feet, courtesy of the title

"Tornado Chick". This was my first true disaster, and I was just fumbling along. I am just a silly girl, not a theological scholar, or a sage. I had no answers. I only possessed my own thoughts and, as it turned out, my behavior when I thought no one was looking.

Late one night, I sat with a new aftermath-friend outside Limbo, drinking coffee and chatting. Suddenly, she changed the subject with an announcement.

"I never totally believed in God. Not that He could love me, anyway."

I quietly responded. "It's okay. He believes in you."

"I think God did this to you."

I leaned down and scratched my dog behind his ears. I was becoming adept at hiding the sudden shock of cold pain in my heart. Certain phrases always made me feel speared with an icicle. I did not argue with her, not because I agreed, but because I could hear something unusual in her voice. It was guilt.

"I've been watching you."

"Okay, that's a little creepy," I grinned.

"See? You can laugh after what happened to you. You help people. You really care about their problems, after what happened to you. I know you hurt. I know you struggle. I see that. But, I also see peace in you, you have hope, after what happened to you! And, you are so ordinary, it's amazing."

I agreed. "There is nothing special about me."

"But, there is! I could not even survive what you have lived through, much less with the... the grace you have."

"Grace?" I laughed. "Allow me to correct that misconception. I'm not remotely graceful. The hope, the love, and the peace you say you see in me, it is not mine. It doesn't belong to me. I cannot even survive this, alone. I am not on my own. It is not my grace that you see. It is His."

"I want what you have. And, I know that you have God. I've been talking to Him lately and I'm going to church on

Sunday. I have a confession, and I don't want you to be mad at me but the tornado might be my fault."

"What?!"

"God did this to you… for me."

I remained silent for just a moment, deciding how I felt about that idea. "He actually does love you that much. And, if that is the case, then for once, I am glad that He did this to me."

I did not know if she was right. I only knew that it was her truth, and that was enough for both of us. "Why?" was a question that many people asked during that time, but it was a luxury that I could not afford. People had their own theories, their own truths, and I allowed that without accepting it as my own. There is nothing wrong with asking why. For me, during one of the few times in my inquisitive little life, "I don't know" was answer enough. There was more than enough to occupy my mind without adding that particular question to the mix.

My email inbox flooded, and I read them all hopefully, but only one mentioned a found dog and she, obviously, was not my Bruce. Though, in my antisocial former life, I had ferociously protected my privacy, I now answered almost every email. I politely responded to the condolences, honestly answered questions, and completely ignored the offers of sex from strangers. Eventually, I changed my email address, thankful that the reporter had advised that I publish only my email address, and not my cell phone number.

During my time in aftermath, I developed a simple set of rules in accordance with my new role of victim. My son and I quickly agreed on "Do not take more than we need, right now." There were too many people affected by this disaster to hoard for the future. When strangers offered furniture, we gratefully declined and suggested they find the victims who currently had housing. This rule paired with another. "People have a need to help. To turn it down out of sheer pride, is unkind. Do not be unkind." As a stubborn, independent, and prideful pair of humans, it was difficult for my little family to follow this rule, but we both tried.

92

Across the street from its foundation, most of our house had been smashed to bits. We differentiated piles of rubble by the room it appeared to have once been. I was digging through the "living room" pile of rubble when I overheard a conversation between my son and one of his friends.

"Dude, I am so sorry this happened on your birthday."

"Don't say that. I'm not sorry. I'm glad! I'm sorry it happened at all, but if this had to happen, I am *happy* it was on my birthday." His voice was rough with sudden emotion. "If it had not been on my birthday, man, my mother would have been home when the tornado hit. My Mom would have been dead on any other day. So, I am ecstatic it was on my birthday. The timing saved my Mom."

It was true. The day of the storm, the family had planned a birthday lunch, but scheduling conflicts changed the lunch to dinner, which was later than I wanted to be out. I liked to be home, settled in with my dogs already fed and walked, by a certain time in the evening. Only special occasions kept me out late, and I generally avoided those for that very reason. James had plans with his friends. I had already given him permission to borrow my car, before our lunch plans changed to dinner plans, and everything else had to be rescheduled, too.

Because of the weather that evening, I had a headache, and I hate driving in the rain after dark. I would have canceled my plans, except it was special plans with my son. I don't watch television, and habitually read in the evenings, instead of listening to the radio. I would have never known the tornado was coming, until it was too late to escape. That specific date on the calendar was the only reason I moved out of the unknown danger, at all. The change in dinner plans was the only reason I moved out of danger in time. Coincidence? Miracle.

I found myself promising upset people that everything would be okay. I did not know how it would be okay, of course, but as I tried to ease the helpless pain in their eyes, I believed it. Though I struggled with my own emotions, in my reassuring others, I never lied. It would be okay, whether I felt like it or not. I did not notice, until someone pointed it out, that I never spoke of a loss without following it with a blessing. I wasn't silver-lining everything. I was reminding them, and myself, of reality. The good deserves equal time, maybe more time than the bad. The truth does not care how you feel in the moment. It is what it is. The reality was "Yeah, this is bad. But, it could have been worse."

CHAPTER NINE

Roadside Eulogy

"The heart has no tears to give."

–Harriet Beecher Stowe

A three-word message, from the man who had once shared my dear dog, made the discomfort of being Tornado Chick completely pointless.

"Bruce is dead."

I called him. He told me where he had found my dog, on the side of the bypass. I had driven by that area countless times, but a pile of brush, recently removed, hid my dog from me. He told me that I did not need to come. He told me that he was certain the dead dog was our dog.

That was not enough for me.

Bruce had been decomposing for days, and, still, I recognized his slightly overweight form from ten feet away. When the dog's "Papa" and I had broken up six months prior, Bruce had moped and I had tried to fill his void with treats, while he tried to fill mine with cuddles. I adored Bruce, and I had retained custody of the dog. In this moment, I desperately regretted that.

Flies covered the well-known heart-shaped white marking on Bruce's black belly. I shooed them away, trying to focus on that, on anything except the fact that my dog no longer had a face. He had faced whatever had killed him, and some impact had shoved his graying muzzle and sensitive face completely into his skull. I informed my breaking heart that Bruce could not have suffered and my heart replied that it, frankly, did not give a shit what I thought. Then, it stubbornly turned away and commenced wailing. I know better than to try to reason with my heart when it gets this way.

Pre-disaster, I was not a hugger, especially when I grieved. When I did initiate a hug during painful times, it was because I felt that I would fall to pieces without human contact. My ex knew this about me. At the loss of Bruce, I tried to hug my former boyfriend and he evaded it. I was not seeking comfort from a former love, or even an old friend. At that point, if it had been Charles Manson standing there, I would have tried to hug him. Charles Manson probably would have hugged me back.

Pre-disaster, I never considered begging for anything. All I wanted to do was fall to my knees and plead with that man to help me, to just let me give my dog a decent burial. Instead, I regained my external composure. There was no reason to fall apart. After all, there was no one there who cared if I did, and I needed to do something with my poor Bruce.

I needed to bury my dog. It was not a desire, but a requirement. I could not, under any circumstances, leave him on the side of the road to be picked up and hauled off to the dump, like unwanted garbage. My car was filled with stuff, not only my salvaged belongings, but those of my son. I could not leave my boy's things lying on the side of the road, risking theft of the little he had left. I asked my ex-boyfriend if he would haul Bruce to my land so I could bury him. He would not even have to touch the decomposing dog; I could do it.

He declined. "He stinks, and is covered in maggots."

I asked if he would put my stuff in his car, so I could fit Bruce in my car, and then follow me home. He did not have time for that. He looked grieved, and said, "Well, I guess the city will come and haul him away." Then, he left.

I sat on the side of the road and shooed flies off my dog, helplessly. I did not know what to do. I could not leave Bruce on the side of the road, not even for a little while. I was stranded. I needed a plan. If my heart would briefly stop that infernal howling, I could think.

I scrolled through my phone until I reached the name of the first animal rescuer on the contact list, and I called Beth. I am not sure how much was intelligible but she got the gist, responding, "I'll make a few phone calls and we will get him off the side of the road soon, I promise. You go ahead and go. You don't need to be there with him. Oh, I am so sorry. The poor dog really doesn't have a face? You go. We will take care of him."

Within minutes, she called me back. "Betti and Dr. G are already on their way. They will take him to be cremated for you. I feel so bad that you had to see him like that. You aren't still there, are you? Did you leave? Tell me you left."

I did. I told her that I was driving as we spoke. As I hung up the phone, I waved a few more flies away from my furry friend's corpse. I tried to think of a few final words to speak over this dog.

This dog had wholly believed himself to be a person. This dog, in the four years that he was my friend, had never once misbehaved. This non-confrontational canine had only shown his teeth twice, and only in defense of his humans. He mothered puppies, as well as his antique little dachshund brother, Buddy. This worrier dog, with sad, hound-dog eyes took his love seriously. He always quickly gave his paw in answer to the question "Are we friends?" with an air of complete commitment, and thumped his tail like mad when I answered my own question with a serious tone, "Yes, sir. We are Best Friends. Yes, sir. Always."

I thought on these things and more, and could not say a word. I could not even tell this faceless dog, one last time, that he was my best friend. I could not speak, and I could not cry, in that moment. There were not enough tears in existence to fully express that particular hurt, so my eyes refused to offer even one.

Bruce's eulogy was the sound of buzzing flies and passing cars.

CHAPTER TEN

Dear God, You Screwed Up. Amen.

"A bruised reed He will not break and a smoldering wick He will not quench."

-Matthew 12: 20

Many of my friends referred to the present site of my former home as Ground Zero. I thought of the area as the Wastelands. Here, I identified the deformed junk that had once been my assets, and inventoried the missing or smashed chunks of my former life. I dug in the rubble, working so hard to trash the remains of prized possessions. I learned to use a sledgehammer to break up our already broken house, and landscaping, into manageable pieces for haul off. We generally just cleared space in the Wastelands for our unknown future.

Every daylight hour, I worked the Wastelands, with family, friends, and strangers. I joked, and I laughed, because gallows humor is my go-to survival mechanism. All the while, I noticed everything. Mementos of my boy's childhood, mementos of my own past, every single item connected to a moment in time. Pieces of my son's baby book, a chunk of kitchen wall that I had proudly painted my favorite shade of blue, favorite coffee cups, the chewed up rawhide and loose collar, belonging to my lost Bruce, the hound who always thought he was human.

The first few days, I cried without really noticing it, but those tears soon disappeared into sweat. My sorrow retreated into silence, refusing to waste itself in expression, and it listened to my jokes without ruining the punchlines. While I threw my things away, without changing expression, mourning busied itself remembering. It was not pain's turn to speak. It could wait.

I inventoried each broken item, and mentally catalogued every attached memory.

"This. This existed. This is no more. Put this away, deep in my mind, and shut that door. Suck it up and do what needs to be done. I will break when the work is finished. If I break now, then I cannot do what is necessary to make my way Home. I will face this loss, later. Now is not the time."

I maintained a notebook of lists of destroyed belongings, and missing items, in accordance with the rules of the insurance company. My Dad & stepmom researched replacement values of everything. My former sister-in-law, Cindy, helped me fill out the property lists. Remembering when and where I originally purchased all of my stuff, as well as what I had paid for it, was a challenge. Furniture, appliances, and clothing, were relatively painless to write down. However, I procrastinated listing the personal items, because my mind would just swerve to avoid my most prized possessions. Finally, there was nothing else left to list.

I handed Cindy the forms and a pen.

"I'll talk. You count. We will knock this out in one session."

I leaned against the kitchen counter and closed my eyes, mentally transporting myself home. As my mind roamed the rooms of my lost home, I would speak to Cindy, in Limbo's kitchen. That was the plan.

I opened the eyes of my imagination, and I was sitting in my old bedroom, on my vanished bed, with the dearly departed Bruce-dog at my feet. The memory was so clear that it seemed I was actually there. My Heart whined and tried to escape that room, but Willpower shoved it back and slammed the creaky-hinged door. Bruce wagged his tail.

I turned my head, looked at all of the things that I will never see again, outside of my own mind. I knew that my body was in Limbo's kitchen, that my sister-in-law waited on the other side of my closed eyelids and I spoke to her. I did not describe the pretty wallpaper border. I did not inform her that the furniture was walnut and formerly belonged to my grandfather before it formerly belonged to me. I did not tell her that my dead dog was in that room with me. I described objects.

"My bedroom." I said flatly. "Black and white waterfall photograph, titled Silent Moods, the first decoration I ever purchased with my own money. I was twelve. We were in Gatlinburg." Always the second item hung on the wall of any bedroom I had ever lived in. I paused long enough for Cindy to calculate the year of purchase and then moved on. I talked fast, faster, rushing through this mental room as quickly as I dared. Hoping to outtalk the terrible pain building in me, to finish before the hurt knocked me to the floor.

"Photos. My brother's wedding picture, gold frame. My grandfather with his fiddle, he was about twenty, then. Man, I hope there is another copy of that, somewhere. Me and Brian, when we were about three and five years old. James and Shadow at Petco. I never printed doubles of that shot. James and I on the Halloween when he went as fireman and I went as a Mom. Another Halloween, James dressed as a Zombie Army man, missing both his front teeth."

Deep breath. No tears, this had to be finished. I kept talking in a dry flood, as Cindy wrote.

"James and Shadow the day we rescued him from the animal shelter. James loved that dog so much. A family photo of your family, Cindy. Baby photos of my nieces, Haley and Madison, two of those. A couple of handmade Mother's Day cards. James spelled 'love' as 'l-u-v-e" on one, and the 's' at the end of his name was backwards on both. Always was, in those days. On the wall above my bed, the plaster impression of James' little baby hand." I paused, and then added very quietly, "I found a corner of that, at the Wastelands, on a little pile of plaster dust."

Leaning against the counter at Limbo, I crossed my arms, literally holding myself together. I peeked at my sister-in-law, to see if she was getting all this, as I did not want to repeat it.

God knew, I would never be able to repeat it. Cindy was sniffling and wiping tears off her cheeks and I shut my eyes tight, again.

I talked my way through, room by room. "Office and playroom. A big Olin Mills family portrait, including my ex-husband. It was not weird to have it there. It made my kid happy to have a picture of his family together. Those Star Wars posters from McDonald's, you know, the ones that went together to form a bigger picture?" I laughed. "I begged everyone I knew to have Happy Meals for lunch so James could have all of those posters. And they did, bless their hearts."

I was shaking. My throat filled up and my voice sounded like I had swallowed sandpaper, but I did not cry. "Living room. A framed poem, "Comes the Dawn" that Mikey's mom gave me as a happy divorce present in 1997. An oil painting of a waterfall. James bought it at a yard sale for three bucks when he was nine. He was so proud of that. Three, no, four, of James elementary school art projects; his mask, my black ashtray..." It was black because the project was to paint a pottery bowl in Mom's favorite color, and James mixed them all since his Mommy liked lots of colors. Black is the color of thoughtful. "...that beautiful, surreal demonic steer painting,..." Childhood art in its purest form.

"…a black and white construction paper heart. According to James, that was a silly color for a heart, since love is always multi-colored…" I trailed off, and then opened my eyes. I could not do any more of this. None of this could be replaced, anyway. My lie was obvious.

"And that's it. That's all there is."

Her lie was also obvious. "And now the hardest part is over."

I stepped outside, allegedly for a cigarette. I needed a minute. I stood in the shadows between a tree and the corner of Limbo, in the darkest part of the night, where no one could see me if they looked. I bit down on my fist, until my knuckles bled, so the neighbors would not hear my sobs. I looked up at the stars, through the tree limbs and the tears that could no longer be contained. I succeeded, somehow, in not making a sound, but I knew that God could hear my spirit wail.

"You didn't take it back, God. Take it back, now, or strike me dead. Please, please. I can't do this, it hurts! I know it's just stuff, but it's more, too. It was my life; it was me. I know that everything is for Your Glory. I know that my job is to glorify You in this. But, You picked the wrong girl! You screwed up, God!"

I squatted on the grass, my hand on the tree for balance. "I'm sorry, I'm so sorry. I want to try, I do. But I cannot honor You in this. I don't know how. It's an official disaster. Have You seen it? Did You look? It's too big and I am just too little. My home is broken. My life is broken. I am broken."

I lay the whole truth, shattered, at His feet. He would have to inventory this damage. "I am not strong enough. I am not smart enough. I am not sane enough. For God's sake, I am not faithful enough! What the hell do You want me to do?"

Then, I listened. The answer did not come from the stars, nor was the response created in my own psyche. It wasn't an audible voice because I am a Christian, not a schizophrenic. The response was a kind and slightly sarcastic echo deep in my soul.

The words were "Who asked you to be those things? I did not. I never have. You have always been convinced that you must be strong, and smart, and brave, all in your own power and abilities. And, my dear child, you have always been wrong about that."

"Then what do I do, Lord?"

"Your job is this. Remember My name. Whatever you need, child, remember My name. Whatever you feel you need to be, child, remember my Name."

God?

Father?

Abba?

Jesus?

 Jehovah?

The list went on.

Then, I understood.

I AM. Whatever you need, child, I AM. Whatever you feel you need to be, child, I AM.

I knew that I was not let off the hook, here. Though God had given me one task, it would be a difficult one for me to accomplish. He was asking me to let go, to surrender everything I had known myself to be, everything, even my day-to-day decisions, to ask, and to trust only Him. It would take practice, struggle, and failures. Possibly, it could take years, or even a lifetime. I hoped that I could complete my journey home before I got it right. If not, I would try, anyway.

CHAPTER ELEVEN

The Thing With Feathers

"And sore must be the storm that could abash the little
bird that kept so many warm."

–Emily Dickinson

At the bottom of my tiny cache of treasured possessions, there is a handwritten sheet of paper. It reads,

"Kevin. Greg. Dee. Cindy. Larry. Shadey. Drew. Curtis. James. Cletis. Jimmy. Danny. Steven. Ryan. Joe. Mike. Stacey. Pat. Shannon. Stephanie. Jenny. Travis. Amanda. Brian. Melody. Dad. Joyce. Mom. Beth. Betti. Jenni. Carol. Beki. Cristie. Debbie. Misty. Tracy. Todd. Tiger. Johnnie. Thomas. Justin. Cassey. Kim. Randy. All co-workers. Dozens of strangers."

The list is dated April 28th, 2011.

One day.

Only one day when hundreds of people were coping with massive losses, and many others had power outages, at least, of their own to deal with.

These people are a few of the miracle-makers who raced to my aid the first day after the end of my world. During this town's vast trouble, these people hurried to help my family. Though I thank the people who said a prayer for me during that time, I love the ones who moved, who hit the ground running. Uncertain of exactly what they could do for me and mine, they did not use uncertainty as an excuse.

They came prepared to try.

I scribbled the list that evening, sure that, in my traumatized mind, I had left out some names. There were so many. But, I tried. By the day after the day after the end of the world, I gave up listing miracle-workers because there were just too many acts of kindness. The love was as overwhelming as the destruction. My cavalry arrived, one by one and in groups. Local businesses, schools, churches, groups, and individuals united so quickly that it was hard to believe this town was unprepared for such a disaster. Lists of resources, places to go for help with meals, shelter, laundry, or computer access, circulated. Every time one of those lists landed in my hands, it just stopped me in my tracks, awestruck by love in action. Churches in Florida sent goods, materials, and people all the way to Tennessee, just to help total strangers. Friends, family, colleagues, former co-workers, friends from high school, and acquaintances from elementary school, all showed up.

They kept coming back.

Next to each name on the miracle list is a sanity-saving act. I doubt that these people were attempting to save me, only help in some small way, but rescue is exactly what they, and all the others, did.

"What do you need?"

"I don't know." They guessed. Breakfast. Dinner. Clothing. Sneakers. Shampoo. Two cold bottles of beer. Necessities.

"Are you okay?"

"I don't know." Hugs. Talk. Silence. Tears. Smiles.

"What can I do?"

"I don't know." They came to my broken neighborhood, armed with chainsaws to clear the devastated landscape, baskets and totes to haul debris, leashes and crates to help me hunt for my missing dogs, and cell phones to call for more assistance.

I lost stuff in that terrible storm. All my friends thought they were bringing was stuff. However, each carried a kind heart and compassionate spirit within and the most important thing each handed to me on the day after the end of my world was Hope.

During disaster clean-up, a friend said, "You know, you have always been the most bull-headed person I have ever known."

I wiped the sweat out of my eyes, and heard the exhaustion in my voice. "Yeah."

"You are obstinate. Difficult. You've never listened to anyone else. You always take the hard road."

Sigh. "Yeah."

"You fight, even when there is nothing to fight against. I think you were a warrior in the womb."

I wondered if she was going to break down all of my character flaws, right there in the middle of my life's wreckage.

"I think that you have spent your entire life in training for this. You are going to make it, girl."

The night after the storm, a friend called and invited me to dinner. In her mind, I was not okay until she actually laid eyes on me. We met at Taco Bell.

"When I heard about what happened to your house, it just blew me away!" She stopped speaking, mortified at her own words.

I cracked up. "Yeah, kind of blew me away, too."

We laughed. We laughed some more. She noticed, despite my genuine laughter, my hands were shaking so badly that I could not hold my food. I was freezing, again, so icy cold for no apparent reason.

We carried our dinner to the parking lot, and sat in her car with the heater running. I was freezing to death at the end of April. Once I warmed up a little, I rolled my window halfway down to smoke.

A man approached. "My wife overheard what you two were saying in the restaurant and I am so sorry. We are heading home to Virginia tonight, so I can't help, but, I thought you could use this. It's all I have on me."

He shoved a brand new plastic wrapped pillow through my partially open window. I exclaimed, "Thank you!" Before I could finish the two-word sentence, a twenty-dollar bill landed in my lap and the guy was gone.

My friend and I looked at each other in shock.

What just happened?" she asked.

"I have no idea," I told her. "But you can turn the heater off now. I'm not cold, anymore."

CHAPTER TWELVE

Words

"The world could do with a good deal more mess, if you ask me."

–Kurt Vonnegut

When people, sympathetically and helplessly, spoke of my tragedy, I countered with hope. I spoke of gratitude and faith, because those existed, and they were as real as the hurt. The simultaneous reality of my loss would just have to wait. When people shed tears for me, I promised them that everything would be okay. I hurt, and I coped. Dealing with my losses would come later, after the sympathetic ones had forgotten.

I found myself listening to the words people used to describe what had happened to me, from their own point of view. In some cases, these perspectives were interesting, other times, amusing. In many cases, I had to learn to forgive the unintentional pain they caused. In the weeks after I became a victim of a natural disaster, everyone asked me the same question. Different people spoke in identically dark tones of pity, sorrow, or the undeniable insinuation that there was nothing to do, not after what had been done to me.

What are you going to *do*, now?

What are *you* going to do, now?

What are you going to do, *now*?

I chose to compose an open, honest letter to my friends, answering this question, all at once, as best I could. As I sat at a donated table, in the kitchen of my Limbo, with a hot cup of coffee brewed in a neighbor's sweet gift, I thought on those words. My life has been a love affair with language, and I realized that the whirlwind had changed many things, including how I defined my world.

"Disaster. Catastrophe. Terrible. Heartbreaking. Pitiful. Gone. Tragedy. Very, very bad. Complete loss... these are words describing the annihilation of the first thirty-four years of my life, in an event that took very little time and did not require my permission, my knowledge or my presence. The little haven I called home for almost a decade, and each of the items I thought of as "mine"- wiped out. In a couple senses of the word, all that remains is my foundation to stand on.

Foundation. There is a word. A beginning, something to build on...like a God who orchestrated several "coincidences" in such a way as to move myself and my son out of the path of the tornado, and who then moved the most amazing people into the path of my subsequent emotional storm. Strangers became friends, while we cried on each other's shoulders. Friends became family, sweating in the rubble, and laughing with me in the face of devastation. Family became a lifeline anchored, as always, in reality.

Reality is another word. The destruction of an old high school yearbook doesn't count for much against the fact that people I haven't seen since high school contacted us to offer help; they showed up and they kept coming back. Losing a plaster impression of my son's baby-hand means little when compared to the warmth and strength of my living child's hand squeezing mine.

Mine. The definition for that word may never be the same. The salvageable pieces of what belonged to me fit in my car, with no return trips for more. One hellish night, my neighbors and I fled at the warning "Another one is coming!" I wore a sweater, my second favorite pair of jeans, and a really cute pair of heels. I ruined my shoes by crawling under downed power lines and over the remnants of homes, so I threw them out. Okay, to be honest, I trashed the shoes in an adult version of the temper tantrum, but they really were quite scuffed. A month later, we have clothing, food, furniture, a place to stay for now (appliances included) and my musician-son has guitars and an amp. My surviving dogs are in safe foster homes. All necessities are accounted for. None of these items, by my old definition, technically belongs to me. But, the love and kindness that placed these things in my possession, that is mine and I will treasure the provision as long as I live. The love makes the bed I sleep in, my bed, and the table where I write this, my table. I have done nothing, ever, to deserve any of this, but those unearned and unrequested acts of human kindness make what is now mine mean more than the possessions I had scrimped, saved, and fought for.

Fight. Now, there is a word I know. Years ago, I fought to get out of debt and improve my credit enough to buy a home. Then, I fought some more, working two jobs to make the payments required to keep that home. I am not prepared to stop fighting now. A natural disaster stole a house I loved, a lifetime worth of earthly possessions packed with beloved memories, those landmarks that made my place recognizable, and killed a very, very good dog. This is my natural response:

"Dear Mister Twister, [insert rude gesture here]."

This experience hurt. I'll live. And, we will go back to the one word which has dragged me through the past weeks; the word that will not allow me to just quit.

Home.

This disaster will become just a part of our story. And I will not forget the words."

CHAPTER THIRTEEN

Walk It Off

"Half the walk is but retracing our steps."

– Henry David Thoreau

My father was a Little League baseball coach. He was good at it, and loved the hobby so much that he continued long past my childhood days. There were many backyard-batting practices in my youth, where our drills included some certain facts of life.

You will get hit with the ball.

It will hurt.

You have two options to deal with the pain:

Suck it up.

Or walk it off.

Crying about it does not help.

Giving up your turn at bat is never an option.

In sorting through the remains of my life, I was hit with the proverbial baseball every other moment. I convinced myself that if I allowed myself to really feel all of it, to dive into a hurt that ran so deep it seemed bottomless, then I would fall apart.

People expected me to fall apart. Some demanded it, and my refusal offended them. They reminded me that falling to pieces was a natural reaction, more than forgivable. But, I felt that I had to hold myself together until I picked up the pieces of everything else. If I allowed a breakdown, then I would be unable to do whatever it was that needed doing.

Falling apart was not an option. I had responsibilities: to myself, to my son, to my dogs who lived in foster-care, to my God, to my family, and to my friends. I became obsessed with my goal: to go home, back to my land. I could not quit. It was my turn at bat.

I noticed what others failed to see. Not only things and memories, but pieces of myself were gone, as well. I had been a writer of stories for as long as I could form letters. I always used words to describe, explore, and deal with my world. When my brain was full of thoughts and emotions, I had always just poured them onto pages. I likened the act of applying words to paper as "just the way I breathe."

I remembered a passing thought I had the night my life blew away. "When madness reaches out to take your hand, it's in the moment you most want to go." The pressure of merely coping, and not dealing, with my trauma built up until I did want to go. I did not have time for insanity. I needed relief, but without a breakdown. I needed to write.

Most of my writings, obviously, were missing. Some disaster volunteers found my most personal of personal missives and took turns reading them, aloud, while standing in a circle like a public poetry reading. I angrily took my poems out of their hands, and later burned each page. I felt violated by the volunteers' actions, though I'm sure they had no such intention. I felt more violated that the privacy I had ferociously guarded for so many years had been turned inside out and scattered god-knew-where.

But, I felt most violated by the fact that, other than a letter or two, lists, or common household paperwork, I could no longer write anything. The words still existed for me, probably more words and stories lived in my brain than at any other point in my life. However, any attempt to release them, via pen, pencil, crayon, or keyboard, led to panic attacks. Panic attacks were a new experience for me, a gift from Mister Twister. In my sudden inability to write, Mister Twister had figuratively stolen my ability to breathe, and in the panic attacks, he had literally stolen my ability to breathe.

When my aching heart threatened to overflow with homesickness for my former life, my mind surpassed its capacity for grief-in-waiting, panic overthrew logic, doubt attacked faith, or the friendly madness (that may have been unrecognized psychological trauma symptoms) tried to hold my hand, I needed relief.

Tears sometimes fell while I was busy doing other things. I would have been embarrassed by this new habit, if it had mattered. Priorities shifted, and appearances had dropped off that list. I had no extra energy to waste on pretending, anyway. When I laughed, cried, grieved, and rejoiced, it was real, even when I did all of the above at the same time.

"Are you okay?"

"Sure." I was.

"You're crying."

I smiled, already used to it. "Oh. Yeah, I do that, now. I seem to have sprung a little leak. I might need a plumber, eventually. But, I really am okay. I'm becoming emotionally ambidextrous."

Crying didn't help. I tried it often enough to be sure, and then extra.

"Suck it up" didn't last. There was too much.

I started walking. Through the wee hours, with my dog, Crash, I paced the silent trailer park or walked the deserted streets. Sometimes Cindy and one of her kids would join me, or my son would walk with me a while. They were silent when I needed them to be, trying hard to understand that my spirit could only be still while my body was moving. When I needed to be alone to pray, they understood that, too. Though my former sister-in-law told me later that she would watch me from her window and cry, as, night after night, I tried to pace and pray my way into equilibrium.

Sometimes I walked for a few hours, and sometimes until dawn. I paced the trailer park, meditating while counting footsteps. I walked random streets in the middle of the night. I walked to my former home, and walked those once familiar roads. I walked late and rarely saw other humans. When I did see people, they never acknowledged my presence. I felt like a spirit.

I couldn't properly explain how the act of moving seemed to press everything in my head back where it needed to be. I thought about where my life had been and where it might now go. I thought of no future further than Home. I walked when there was too much to say, and I walked when I couldn't speak at all.

At the very least, I figured that I would end up with the nicest legs in the sanitarium. But, as it turns out, I keep my sanity in my shoes.

CHAPTER FOURTEEN

Popsicle Sticks and Blueprints

"It isn't what we say or think that defines us, but what we do."

-Jane Austen

I perched on a new-to-me wooden chair in Limbo's kitchen, reading an email on a donated laptop. A stack of house-building books towered on my right, with an open "For Dummies" topping the stack. Most of the table was covered with scattered, pencil drawn, house plans, pages of options, and notebooks full of numbers. Numbers and numbers and numbers confirmed that my insurance policy was not anywhere near enough to re-build. I could not afford to go home.

The email I read was a polite, sympathetic, and informative response from a representative of Habitat for Humanity, a reply to my inquiry about the possibility of the organization helping me re-build my home, on my land. It was an option, a possible way home, but the requirements included a catch. The insurance company had paid off my land, and Habitat required that I sign over the land to them, to be included in the mortgage. Which was not an unreasonable request, but I hesitated.

I pulled my land deed from an envelope on the cluttered table, and held it, praying for guidance. A line from my "promise of home" Scripture, "For I have given it (the land) into *your* hands" entered my mind, and held, there. My fingers traced the paper. The land was in my hands, and I would not put this deed into anyone else's hands. I must keep the land in my own grip.

I must trust God to send me home. Even when I could not see how it could be managed, even when I was so homesick and desperate to be there as soon as possible. Even when my heart filled with impatience, I must behave as if I trusted

Him. Even when I could not control my thoughts, or my doubts, I could still choose to behave as if He was in control.

I slowly typed a short, polite refusal to Habitat's kind offer of help. As disappointed tears dripped onto the keyboard, my fingers slipped on the keys.

As I denied one option, another one arrived. There was a house across town set for demolition, and the owner offered the option of moving the entire house, within two weeks, onto my land as part of the sale package. The deal looked good, the price was reasonable, and the timeframe was exactly what I wanted.

I had just begun grocery shopping when the owner called me. I left my buggy and stepped into the parking lot to take the call. He was apologetic, and upset. "While I was offering to sell you the house, my partner was offering it to another family. My partner and I are arguing but I insist that you get first choice. He should have told me that..."

I interrupted. "Can you hold on a second, sir?" I walked around the corner of the building, so that I would be completely alone. I covered up the phone with my hand, looked up at the blue sky, and said, softly, "Hey, God, it's me. You've got this situation under control, right?"

Then, I spoke into the phone, with certainty. "Sir. Offer the house to the other family. If they don't, won't, or can't buy it, then I will know it is meant for me...No, sir, I insist. Thank you for calling."

I hung up, and sighed. More than anything, I wanted to go home, yet I persisted in turning down every option to get there. Had I lost my ever-loving mind? Maybe. I went back to my grocery shopping.

Though the miracle of funding had still not materialized, I spent evenings teaching myself to draw house plans. I chose my favorite idea, though it seemed as if I was painstakingly drawing a castle in the air. I would gladly accept any dwelling God chose to bestow upon my family, but I dreamed to occupy my mind.

I showed my former sister-in-law and my youngest nephew my ideal house drawing. Three bedrooms, one designated as the Music Room, two bathrooms, a kitchen island, a tiny laundry room off the kitchen, an open floor plan, and just a little bigger than my former, beloved home. I didn't care for fancy. Cindy flipped through my stack of house-building and design books.

"Have you figured out how you can afford to re-build?"

"Nope. But, God promised that I could go home, so, I better be ready."

"Did He say when?"

"No, and I wish I had asked. It could take decades. I'm afraid that it will take decades."

"Why don't you ask Him?"

"Because I don't think that is how this game is played. I get the feeling that is against the rules, right now."

"Can you ask Him how?"

I laughed, "Oh, I have. About a hundred times a day."

"But, you are certain that you are going to get to go home, eventually."

I loved that sister of mine, mostly for her facial expression when she made that statement. She did not think that I was crazy.

"Absolutely! And, I am willing to do whatever it takes. I just have to find a cheap enough building method. But, I am going home, even if I have to build a house with my bare hands, out of popsicle sticks."

My young nephew, who had been listening silently, spoke up. "How many popsicles would you need to eat?"

I grinned, and then quickly assumed a serious expression. "A lot. And you, young man, are in charge of the popsicles. You better get to work. I've got a house to build."

His smile was beautiful as he headed for the freezer.

CHAPTER FIFTEEN

The Tithes

"Your suffering comes at such a high cost. Don't waste it."

-Jimmy Larche

During the last of a series of meetings, where a stranger and the rules of an insurance policy would determine the total price of my life, my father sat beside me. I stared at the round table, wondering how much human grief it had seen divvyed up into dollars. My father read my mind, "Most people are never told how much their life is worth. Generally, this kind of thing happens after a funeral."

Dad had joined me in this meeting with my insurance man for an important reason; he was not by my side for moral support but to keep me from doing anything stupid.

The insurance company had already given me a small check to cover "the refrigerator", food and kitchen items that would need to be replaced prior to The Payoff. My mother had inventoried my missing fridge, in order to come up with a price that matched the "fridge check." I had reviewed her list the night before the big meeting, and corrected it.

"Mom, really? Three pounds of steak? I have never had three pounds of steak in my freezer in my life, much less at the same time. I'm changing this to a pound of turkey burger."

"But the total needs to match the check they already gave you, or you will have to give some back. We need to exaggerate what you remember owning, just a little, to make up the difference for what you have forgotten to mention. It will even out."

It was a logical argument, and one that Dad, my stepmother, Joyce, and my brother had already tried to explain to me. I understood the point. It was sensible. Everybody did it. Yet, it still seemed dishonest. My perspective was that I was an honest person, and there was no point in even having a moral code, if I only followed my personal code when it did not hurt me to do so.

So, my father drove me to the meeting to attempt to keep my morality from ruining me financially.

The insurance man peered over the fridge list at me. "You know, this total is a bit less than the check I already wrote to you."

"Yes, sir. I didn't have that much in my fridge," I responded.

I could sense my father considering slamming his head on the table in frustration.

"You know you owe me money back, now."

"Yes, sir."

The insurance man looked at me as if I had sprouted an extra nose. "Why didn't you just make things up, to cover for what you don't remember to list?"

I did not dare glance at Dad.

I explained my moral code to the insurance man. He listened and read my list, probably noticing where I had scratched items out. Then, he suddenly asked, "Did you have salt and pepper? Spices?"

"Not in the fridge. But, yeah, of course."

"You had food in your cabinets. I'm guessing it was enough to equal the check, so we are even there."

I opened my mouth to argue, but Dad nudged my leg with his foot. This was why he had come along. I closed my mouth and nodded.

The insurance man reviewed my list. "Stuffed animals, 1977 to 2011. 1977?"

My big brother had bestowed his brand new teddy bear upon his brand new baby sister. All through our childhood, my mother would have to sneak the toy into the wash, and return it before bedtime, because I refused to sleep without Beary. I passed my old bear on to my own son, who loved the battered bear but outgrew it, too, and decided to donate the bear to the less fortunate. At that time, his Mom had approved his sweet gesture of passing on a beloved toy, but then, caving to her internal childish ultimatum, secretly rescued the old bear from the donation box and hid it in her closet.

Mister Twister stole my teddy bear. The replacement price for Beary was five dollars.

We quickly reviewed the rest of my property lists and he handed me a check. It wasn't much for what I had in mind, going Home, but it was still more money than I had ever seen.

Dad said something about a pretty good down payment on a new mortgage. He still believed my best option was to buy a house and start over, elsewhere.

The insurance man shook my hand and thanked me for my honesty, something he did not see much of. "Now that you have your money, you can start to re-build like you planned."

Dad glared at him. "Don't encourage her."

"Oh, um, you can go shoe-shopping now, or whatever you like!"

I laughed.

After depositing the check, I headed back to Limbo to plan the disbursement of funds. I had already done the math. It would not be enough to rebuild, and my credit was not good enough for a building loan. On a sheet of paper, I began breaking down the money. I split the personal property insurance funds fairly between myself and my son. Then, I had a thought. Even when I had been a churchgoer, I had never tithed. I preferred to consider "tithing" to include time, gifts, and talents, instead of just money. But, now, I actually had some money and I felt that I owed God his part of it. However, donating it all to a church did not feel right.

I decided to send part to the only church I ever felt truly comfortable attending, Faith Connection, and save the rest to spend on others, as God led, over the next several months.

The first person who I felt moved to help was easy, as she was a close friend. I secretly paid her late utility bill and a month of her rent. It was fun, especially the secretive part.

When someone I had a rough history with approached me for help, I did not hesitate when I felt God's nudge, because we had already tried to put our past behind us, and learned to be civil to each other.

I was in a position to help those I held some love for, even if the love had been in my past. I did not help everyone I cared about, but those who I felt led to assist. When I could do so anonymously, I did it that way because this was not about my own altruism. It was about learning obedience, and about how I served God. I did not want credit.

Obedience is kind of like that moral code I mentioned. It does not count when it is easy. When the tithing challenge arrived, I almost failed.

God laid an old acquaintance's troubles on my heart, a nice fellow from my youth, who I had seen a couple of times in recent months, but not a person I ever spent much time with. I did not know him well enough to find a way to help ease his troubles anonymously, and a direct encounter, involving free money, would be awkward. I hesitated to help him, partly because he had grown into a good-looking man. People would think I was helping him because of that "womanly manipulation" generalization. Certainly and absolutely not the case, but I was sure that I would come across as some crazy, infatuated psycho-stalker, offering a sum of money for no apparent reason.

God worked on my heart, and I countered with the certainty that he, his family and friends, would maintain the wrong idea about my intentions. I did not feel comfortable asking him to keep the gift a secret, because that would seem more insane and strange.

One night, I paid the bills and went to bed with the knowledge that I had never once managed to pay all my bills at the same time, and still have money left over for groceries, until now. It was a nice feeling. It was a secure feeling. It was a safe feeling.

I

Felt

Awful.

How was it fair that I was in my bed, without a financial care, while my acquaintance, a truly good person, worried over his own problems? He had worries that I had the capacity to ease a bit, at least to offer hope that God loved him, was looking out for him, and had not forgotten his trials. And, I had divine orders to do just that.

Yet, I tossed and turned for hours, countering the truth of what I should do with one question. What would people think of me, if I did this?

What would people think?

My brain began, randomly, connecting dots that were separated by decades. This particular man needed help. This particular man had a brother. When I got pregnant in high school, in the Bible Belt, people had spurned me. I remembered only one instance when someone ignored my Scarlet Letter and actually initiated a friendly conversation with me. That teenage boy, my acquaintance's brother, had treated me as a human, when no one else would because I was sixteen and pregnant. The age I had been, sixteen, was when most people had avoided me and my newfound bad reputation, at best, or left notes in my school locker, calling me terrible names; that was the age I had been when I vowed to

Never

Care

What

People

Thought.

I realized, at age thirty-four, that I had not really cared about other people's bad opinions of me since my sixteen-year-old self had decided against it. The dots connected; I saw the picture.

And, I suddenly knew that the intrusive thought stopping me from obeying God's will, and helping this very nice guy, could not be my own. There was no way. I had not cared what people thought about me for eighteen years. "What will people think?" Now? Who cared? I did not even know this guy's friends and family. For that matter, I hardly knew him. How could their opinion affect me?

I stumbled out of bed, at two o'clock in the morning, filled out a check, and scrawled my signature and the word "tithes" on it. I contacted my acquaintance and requested his address later that morning, without telling him why I wanted it. Then, I purchased a greeting card, and stuffed the check inside.

As I dropped the card in the post office mailbox, I thought, "Okay, God, I am being obedient. Other than him perceiving me as an insane woman, and never speaking to me again, what's the worst that could happen?"

As the metal door slammed shut behind my, now en route, tithe, I prayed. "I'll accept the appearance of the crazy, psycho-stalker for you, Lord. Just, please, don't let me end up with a restraining order filed against me, okay?"

CHAPTER SIXTEEN

The Writing on the Wall

"The soul helps the body, and at certain moments, it raises it. It is the only bird that sustains its cage."

–Victor Hugo

Hard labor in the rubble of what was my beautiful home by day, and hours of walking at night, had exhausted me beyond my physical and mental capabilities. The little kitchen table at Limbo was covered with books, house plans, budgets, and loan requirements. My brain was full and the result of all my research was, still, "impossible". My very soul was sore. My faith was diminishing by the moment.

I wanted to go home. No, I needed to go home. God had promised me, but the joy in the given promise faded in the absence of a timeframe for it to be kept. Faith cringed at the thought of years, waiting and working, for fulfillment.

My son was at a friend's for the night. By eleven o'clock, Crash was asleep at my feet. I was drunk. It had been two months of nonstop labor, only two months though it seemed a lifetime already. The lost decade of my life welled up in my mind, as tears welled in my eyes. I should walk. I should walk until the memories were stomped back down into the bottom of my mind. How long could I hold the agony down? How long could I hold it in, when there was no end in sight? I should walk. I was too drunk to walk. I should stagger. I didn't get up.

I sat on the couch and stared at the blank kitchen wall. The previous tenant had painted that wall with dry-erase paint. "I give up, God," I prayed, "I quit. I'm not going home. I'm too tired." Despair is dangerous. I could almost hear it, running at me, as if it had been waiting for those very words. It sounded like a terrible wind, and I knew that what little remained of me would blow away if it caught me.

I jumped to my feet, startling Crash, and stumbled to the kitchen wall. I grabbed a dry-erase marker and scrawled, "Arise, let us go up against them. For, we have seen the LAND, and, indeed, it IS very GOOD. Would you do nothing??? DO NOT HESITATE to go, that you may enter to possess the LAND. When you go, you WILL come to a secure people and a large land. For GOD HAS GIVEN IT into YOUR HANDS, a place where there is NO LACK of anything that is upon the earth! Judges 18: 9&10"

I paused, breathing hard, trying to contain my sobs. I underlined the word "land" three times, for each of the three repetitions. My land, MY land. God didn't forget the decision I had humbly asked Him to make. God didn't forget the promise He had made to me in those words of scripture.

I would not forget. I could not let myself forget.

I erased the words.

I scrawled them again, in larger letters.

I wrote them.

I erased.

I wrote, in blue dry-erase. Over and over, trying to burn the blue words into my brain. I wrote, and I cried, read them aloud, erased, and did it again. This was beyond a memorization exercise. I needed those words to be seared onto my brain and my soul. When I could not believe, I needed to remember that the promise was still true. When the marker stopped working, I threw it across the room, grabbed a red marker, and kept writing. When the pressure I put on the red marker shoved its tip up into the marker body, I switched to green. Over and over, I scrawled God's words on the wall of Limbo.

I did not know how long I repeated those two verses, in the sheer desperation to avoid losing the promise of my God. I had started at eleven. It seemed that about forty-five minutes had passed. By the time I sank into a chair, allowing the marker to fall out of my numb hand, my shoulder was aching, my right arm was sore, my eyes were dry, I was sober, and suddenly, completely calm.

It was four o'clock in the morning.

I didn't know when the promise would be fulfilled. My time no longer mattered. All that mattered was that it would be fulfilled, in His time.

That was enough.

I rested my head on the wooden table. "Please, God, just let it be enough."

CHAPTER SEVENTEEN

Excuse Me, but You're in My Road

"Your ears shall hear a word behind you, saying, "This is the way, walk in it."

–Isaiah 30: 21

Two months working the wastelands, and living in Limbo. Two months, hanging on to my faith until my fingers ached. Two months, coping with a trauma, and the exhaustion of not taking time to deal with it. Two months of homesickness, for that lost place in the world that was mine, and for the unknown person I could become, once this was over.

Mom and I went to a nearby town to look at a few manufactured homes. Several were nice, but my favorite contained three bedrooms, and two baths, with an open floor plan and a kitchen island. I did not notice the similarity to my "castle in the air" layout. In fact, I did not notice it until years later. When I eventually compared the drawing of my dream home with the actual catalog layout, I also noticed what the advertising folk had named it. The Game Changer.

I asked the owner's wife, who was showing me the homes, the only two questions I cared anything about. "How much will it cost?" and "How long will it take?"

She started the spiel about options, as they could order colors and such, per my specifications. She said that because of material shortages, she could not give me a timeframe on delivery.

I did not even think of my question.

It never once crossed my mind to ask.

Until I heard my own voice say, "No, I mean, how much is the one we are standing in? You're going to sell me the display."

The saleslady turned to stare at me. My mother turned to stare at me. If I was not trapped in my own skin, I would have turned to stare at me, too. I had blurted something completely ludicrous.

The saleslady began, "I cannot sell you the display. This is a good seller, and we could not even show it, again, until another display arrived. I just can't...Okay."

I stared at her. My mother stared at her. If she was not trapped in her own skin, she would have stared at herself, I think.

After she changed her mind, midsentence, we walked out of my display model, toward the office. Mom whispered to me, "Something weird happened in there."

I just pointed at the heavens and we smiled.

A few minutes later, I was in a meeting with the owner. I told him the maximum that I could afford for a down payment, which was about half of what I had left from the insurance payoff. After all, my family had to replace everything we had ever owned, not just the house. The gentleman pulled up my credit report, & frowned. "Your credit score is not good enough. I can't sell anything at all to you."

"What? I mean, I know it isn't great, but does it say why?"

"This says that you missed a couple of mortgage payments." He gave me the timeframe. After the house was destroyed, the mortgage company had informed me that they were going to take the insurance payoff, and for me to stop making payments. I explained this. He said that I could call and fix my credit, but it could take quite a bit of time. He offered to do it for me. What he could not do was sell me a home, not with the down payment I offered, not even at a higher interest rate.

"What else can you do?"

"Honey, I don't think…"

I stood up, speaking firmly, "I am going to need you to think of a way. And, I'll think, too. I am going home. This is the path that I am taking to get there. I AM going home and…" Passion lowered my voice to an intimidating whisper, "it is not a good idea for anyone to get in my road. You sir, are currently in my road, and I am giving you the opportunity to move out of my way." He did actually look a little intimidated. Oops. "Think about it. Call me later. Thank you and have a nice day."

That evening, he called to tell me that he had worked some numbers and the only way was a bigger down payment. Was that okay with me? I responded that I had to crunch some numbers of my own.

I prayed and reviewed my estimates. We would have no appliances, furniture, clothing, or anything, at all. Every single thing had to be purchased again, and I had already decided not to purchase anything brand new. A down payment of almost half my funds was really all I could afford, unless I dipped into my tithe money, but that was not mine to spend. I was not going to steal from God.

I flipped through the lined pages in the little cashbook I had titled "The Replacement Game" and felt God's little nudge.

Double the down payment.

I looked at the long, expensive list of everything I would have to buy for my family to return to normal, and hesitated.

Double it and trust Me.

I closed the book, and dialed the phone. The conversation took five minutes. The interest rate was outrageous, but the mortgage would only be ten years, and my land would remain in my hands, alone. By the time I hung up, I was on my way home and the road was clear.

HOME, THE SEQUEL

CHAPTER EIGHTEEN

A Box to Place a Bed

"Toto, I have a feeling we're not in Kansas, anymore."

–L. Frank Baum

Home, the Sequel, took a full month to set up.
Paperwork had to be done, funds transferred, property lined surveyed, and power and water lines dug. It was a long thirty days, a flurry of activity and waiting. Almost home was a place all its own, and every day it grew harder for me to remain under control. It was not simply a matter of impatience, or even frustration. The closer I got to Home, to giving myself permission to break, to stop coping with my

trauma, and finally, to begin dealing with it, the more overwhelmed I was by each day.

At some point, I scribbled "Eighty nightmarish days. One thousand, nine hundred, and twenty hours of Hell and Limbo. Now, I wait for only a moment. One moment, that I can call Now, the moment tomorrow might begin."

One house in my neighborhood had been re-built. Mine would be the second. The view from my Promised Land was a wasteland of emptiness and destruction. The houses I had been accustomed to seeing for a decade were still in various stages of clean up, or the owners had just abandoned the rubble. I certainly could not blame them. Who wanted our memories?

It hurt to see my land torn up, first by Mister Twister, and then again, by the men who I had hired to bulldoze my foundation, the sole survivor of Then, the home that was. That foundation had to be destroyed to make room for the new place. The Sequel was a lifesaver, a game changer, a miracle, and also a place that was mine because I purchased it, not because it spoke to my soul. I was so grateful for my upcoming Sequel, but I did not love it. I just desperately needed a box to place a bed. This would be the wrong house, but in just the right place. Once there, and only there, I could fully grieve my loss. Knowing that it was so close, and still, with no date set for my return home, my pain insisted on swelling, heavy and threatening. My loss demanded to be fully faced, while I insisted on only looking at it out of the corner of my eye; it had been ugly a couple of months ago, and had grown monstrous. In those final thirty days, I battled it, pleading, and placating. "Not yet, not yet, not yet. I am almost home. I can make it." If I could only hold the pieces of me together long enough.

The final setback, the last long waiting period, the very last thing we needed was power. The timeframe, for weeks, had been "any day, now". Any day now, I reminded my grief, which was trying to get my full attention. Daily, I stopped to visit my empty, waiting, new home. I had doubled the down payment on this place, and I could not even live in it. Since I had decided to spend the money I planned to use on furniture on the house, itself, there was no reason to shop. In fact, there was no need to shop, as my family and friends furnished the Sequel. As was my habit, I entered the silent house, made sure the breakers were on, flipped on the air, and listened, hopefully, for the sound of the central air unit running. Silence. Disappointed again.

I opened all the windows and wandered aimlessly around the house. I tried not to cry as I looked at the gifts of furniture. My loved ones had chosen well. I picked up a pretty, cream lamp, and it joined me on my sad little voyage across the room, as I tried to decide if the lamp would prefer living in a different corner. I spotted an outlet, nowhere near a table, and on a whim, I knelt and plugged in the lamp.

The bulb lit. Still kneeling, holding the lamp aloft, I shrieked, quite loudly, in utter joy, "Thank you, thank you, thank you, my Lord!" It was no longer a pretty furnishing, but the most beautiful sight my sore eyes could see. I cried, and I laughed, and I praised God, aloud. I fell prostrate on the floor, still holding the lamp above my head, as I sobbed, laughed, and praised. I raised myself to my knees, staring at the bright lamp held high in my hands, and I kept laughing and praising God.

I heard a small voice, then, and the voice said,

"What the hell is she doing?"

I turned my head and looked directly through the open window, at a few construction workers, looking in at me. I lowered the lamp, realizing that I appeared to be one mad, lamp-worshipping lady. I went to the window, and considered messing with their minds a bit, but I was just too happy for fun. I called, "My power's on. WE ARE COMING HOME!"

Those sweet gentlemen dropped their tools, grinning, and applauded.

I called my son, at Limbo. He sounded at least three-quarters asleep. "Hi, honey, what are you doing?"

"Taking a nap."

I could not wipe the smile off my face. "Well, no rush, just when you finish your nap and have time, will you do me a little favor?"

A yawn. "Sure, Mama. What is it?"

"Start packing your stuff."

"What?"

"It's time to go home, my love."

Through the phone, I heard him hit the floor, running. It was a five-minute drive to Limbo, if you failed to apply traffic laws. When I arrived, my strong and brave man-child, wide awake and eyes shining, waited. He clutched a single, full, trash bag in one hand, and a donated guitar in the other. His possessions were packed and he was ready for Home, too.

CHAPTER NINETEEN

Storm Damage

"Nothing is so painful to the human mind as a great and sudden change."

-Mary Wollstonecraft Shelley

When my man-child was "my little man", not very long after we purchased Home, the Original, he determined my eternal resting place. As I sipped my coffee, I watched my little man standing under our largest tree, looking up into the branches, obviously thinking hard. He finally nodded to himself, and joined me on the carport.

"Mama, do you see that tree?"

He pointed to the largest tree in the yard, nearest the house.

"I think that one is the Mom to all the other trees."

I did not point out the flaw in his theory, that our trees were different types. I loved my son's thought processes, and his observations. I just replied, "You think so?"

"Yeah, see, it is the biggest, so it is the oldest, and it towers over the other trees. It is looking over them all, protecting them, like a Mama and her tree-children. Do you see?"

I leaned over, pressed my cheek against the top of his sun-warmed head, sneaking in a hug, and looked at the trees framing our property's patch of sky from his perspective.

"I see it." I did.

"Mama, you are twenty-five. That's pretty old." I laughed at the seemingly sudden change of subjects. But, knowing my child, I knew that the trees and my decrepitude would be connected, if I waited.

"You are going to die." He patted my hand, consolingly. "Not now, but when I'm all grown up and you are really old."

I hid a smile. "Like thirty-five, Mister Random?"

"When I'm a grown-up man, and you are old and dead, will I still live here?"

"If you like, you will live here. The house will be yours then, but you can live wherever you please." I watched his expression, listening to what he was saying, as well as listening for what he was not saying.

"Where will you live, Mama?"

"When I die of old age, in a very long time, I have a reservation in Heaven. And, when you die, in a very, very long time, you will meet me there."

"I know. But, I'm just thinking." I so loved when he was "just thinking."

"You might get bored in Heaven, after a while. You'll want to go on vacation, and visit me, even if I can't see you." He pointed at the tree. "Do you think your soul would like to live in that Mama-tree when you are on vacation from heaven? You'll get to be Mama to me and the little trees, then. You'd like that. You love it here and you'll be close to me."

I heard what he did not say, then. "I think that tree would be the most perfect vacation house for your Mama's soul, buddy, especially because I'll always be close to you."

A decade later, I sat on what was left of my carport, and waited while a different, grown-up man looked up at the Mama-tree. This man was the professional tree-guy, and his job was to determine the storm damaged tree's fate.

This man, also, nodded to himself, the universal sign of a completed thought process. I joined him at the base of the Mama-tree, looking up at her twisted limbs, already weathered gray at the points where the branches were ripped violently away.

"I advise you go ahead and cut it down, before it falls down. Do you see how the leaves are still green there? It is not dead, but it is very damaged. There is a chance that it can come back, but it is unlikely to survive such a shock."

My heart wanted to correct him. The correct word was "she", not "it" and she was supposed to be my soul's vacation spot, someday. I maintained silence, carefully listening to the professional's assessment, and then told him I would think on it.

I sat in the dirt under the Mama-tree for a while, looking at the newly shattered branches framing the patch of blue sky belonging to my empty land. She was still the Mama-tree, to me, though all five of the yard's smaller trees, her children, were missing. The twin pines, the crabapple-home for caterpillars, the heavenly scented cedar that sang in cicada season, and James' front-yard climbing tree had all been torn away.

The tree-guy's professional assessment of Mama-tree's damage resembled the general opinion, post disaster, about my own chances. Shock. Trauma. Wounded. Scarred. Unable to thrive, again. Might survive, but the damage was forever irreparable. Might live, but never come back as before.

When the Mama-tree had been whole, she was my soul's future vacation spot. Wounded and shredded, she reminded me of my spirit, now. I decided that it was only fair to allow my sole remaining tree to fight for her life. After all, I intended to fight for mine.

I placed my hand on the tree, with my palm on her bark, and my fingers covering a gash in her tree-skin. I prayed sincerely for the Mama-tree's healing. Her storm damage somehow resembled my own, and I hoped that if she could take her life back, then so could I.

As time passed for both of us, Mama-tree sprouted new leaves on her few remaining branches. There was still beautiful life in an ugly broken old tree. She was winning her fight. Her broken appearance would have been a daily reminder of my disaster, except that my own existence was already one. We were both forever changed, but as she showed signs of growth, they mirrored my own. I never grew leaves, of course, but I got sappy with my loved ones. I even became a bit of hugger, for special people.

When the time to plant children for Mama-tree arrived, I decided to plant a special one in honor of our lost Bruce. I had not been able to speak a word in my intense grief over his death, and though he had been cremated, I still felt the urge to bury my dog, somehow. I needed a farewell, and I needed the memory of Bruce to be a part of life without him.

How I had adored looking into Bruce's expressive, loving yet sad, hound-dog eyes. Whenever he crossed my mind, my heart still wept, and always would. I chose a specific type of tree with these things in mind.

As I shoveled away earth to make room for the young Weeping Willow, months after the loss of my hound dog, I cried as if I were digging a grave. As I dropped his favorite flavor of rawhide bone, barbeque, into the empty hole and then covered it with the tree, I remembered the feel of his paw in my palm. I whispered his belated eulogy to the child-tree. I only needed five words.

"Best friends. Yes, sir. Always."

CHAPTER TWENTY

The Deal with Mustard Seeds

"...if you have faith as a mustard seed, you will say to this mountain, 'Move from here to there', and it will move"

-Matthew 17:20

Nightmares plagued me, and being awake did not keep them at bay. The term is flashback, but for me, it was more of a splitting. I was just smoking an afternoon cigarette with a friend, for example, but it was also night, and I was climbing over power lines, watching my step, looking for bodies, seeing the space my home occupied, now occupied by emptiness. And, the wind was blowing, again. But, this time, I would die.

I was there, again. I was then, again. It took all of my focus just to stand still and smoke that cigarette, and all of my willpower to avoid reacting to what I, alone, saw. While the daytime me pretended that night did not exist, simultaneously, I prayed the friend would not notice.

Sometimes, my friend said, "Are you cold? You're shaking."

Sometimes…, no, I cannot use that word. It isn't true.

Not sometimes, but often…,

Actually,

almost always,

I lied.

"Yes. I'm just cold." And, when my friends offered their jackets, I wore them.

The inability to control my own mind humiliated me, and because I had watched my grandmother suffer and die with Alzheimer's disease, I was terrified by it. I kept the secret, because I was also ashamed of the fear, in all of its forms.

In the Christian community, the standard response to a trial is "Have faith." When suffering continues, the solution is "Have more faith." Fear not, saith the Lord. With God, there is no room for fear. That's what they say. With faith the size of a mustard seed, I expected to move mountains. I had at least that much faith, probably a little more, and I did not even want to relocate an anthill.

I only wanted to stop seeing things that were not there. A divine shield from reliving the night the bottom dropped out of the sky was not too much to request. It would be such a tiny thing for my Almighty, about the size of a mustard seed.

Yet, the nocturnal reappearances of the storm and the daylight nightmares of its handiwork continued unabated.

This is the deal with faith like a mustard seed. Yes, God can relocate mountains with it. Sometimes, it is not the mountain that needs to be moved.

I never felt that God was unconcerned with my state of mental disrepair. I am His child. Although, even now, I have no claim to any knowledge of why He did not take my pain away, I do theorize, and the theory feels like truth. His concern was for more than just my psychological damage.

I have always been a bit of a meddler toward God and my circumstances.

"Hey. Hey, God, what are You doing? Can I help? I can help. I'll do this. This will help." Maybe, God wanted me to sit still and just let Him love me.

Maybe, I did not need my trauma to disappear. I just needed to be held through the hurt and the terror. I have always considered myself a strong woman. In fact, I demanded it of myself. Whenever I hurt, I always just wanted to be left alone, and whenever I failed, I even wanted God to leave me alone to the consequences of my mistakes.

When I woke from those nightmares, still entangled in both the horror of my memories and the dread that my new life would always be this way, He did not just have His hand on me. Like a little child, I crawled into my Father's lap, sobbing in His arms, and allowed Him to hold me until I cried myself back to sleep.

No one else could go with me to that place in my life. No one else could have loved me through that monstrous fear, terrible anger, and overwhelming doubt. That is when God does His best work. He already knew that He could love me through anything. He already knew that He would hold me through anything.

Maybe, I had to learn to allow Him to do this.

With God, there is no room for fear. That's what they say. This is what they imply; that fear is a failure and doubt is a fault and God cannot handle either. This implication makes God a bit of a wimp.

My God is tougher than that.

CHAPTER TWENTY-ONE

Resurrection Pains

"To be able to forget means sanity."

–Jack London

After moving into the Sequel, we threw a homecoming party for those who had helped us in so many ways, and then dug in for the next marathon, damage repair. Pages and pages of the Normalcy Project had to be crossed off the list.

Also, there was the part of damage repair that few guessed. I had coped with my trauma for the past few months, pretty well, according to my friends. Of course, their standards were not very high, under the circumstances. Now, it was time to deal with it.

As guests left the homecoming party, they said, "You're okay, now. It's all over." I knew better, but I chose not to enlighten them.

The storm was not over for me. In ways, it had just begun. As the acknowledged but unaddressed emotional trauma grew, I was becoming a storm in a teacup and felt that it was my responsibility to avoid allowing others to take a sip. In part, I determined this in order to avoid the unwanted persona of victim that others consistently insisted on forcing on me.

Also, since the tornado, I had been re-introduced to a humankind that I had never thought much of, a society that I avoided when possible. Because people often suck. The masses of thoughtful acquaintances, and the uncounted kindnesses of strangers, showed me an essence of humanity that I had previously believed practically mythical. Suddenly, I loved people very much. They had supported and protected me, and now it was my turn.

I was home, on my promised land, and there was great joy in being here. I knew that the joy could not be true, however, until I faced everything I had lost. I admit that I did not deal nearly as well as I had coped. Most of my support system had returned to their everyday lives, believing that, for me, it was all over. I allowed them to believe.

In the evenings, after work, I worked on my land's storm damage and then on my own. One of my coping mechanisms during aftermath was the active mantra of Never Stop Moving, and though my manic work ethic continued at the Sequel, I now permitted myself to think. The mental inventory of memories and heartbreak, that I had shoved into the back of my mind during my time in Limbo, could not just be picked up and considered individually. Once I opened the door that I had stomped shut during my hours of walking, there was no closing it, and no way to stem the onslaught of grief

My quiet crazy grew. Panic attacked me, for no apparent reason, more often and the repetitive nightmare of my home's destruction increased its terror nightly. Thunderstorms sent me into fetal position and I could not bear the smallest breeze to blow in my face. Driving home was agony, as each reminder of the tornado I passed served to convince me that when I drove over my hill, the Sequel would not be there. Every ordinary day held the real possibility of disaster, because it had been just an ordinary evening when catastrophe struck. Every day, as I pulled into my driveway, I was filled with both gratitude and disbelief at the simple existence of my house, right where I had left it. I could not leave the house if my dogs were inside. If it rained while I was in town, I raced home, to verify that home was still there.

The growing conviction, that I could count on nothing to remain as it was, spread. As I walked into a store, I was already planning an alternative strategy to get myself home, in case my car disappeared from the parking lot. I could not bring myself to fill out my planner more than a day at a time, and that day was always today.

My boss tried to make plans with me, and advised that I write down the plans so I would not forget.

I opened my planner, shook my head, and closed it.

"I can't write it down. It's too far away," I admitted quietly.

He shut the office door. "What's going on? What's on your mind?"

"I do not believe in tomorrow. Like, at all. What I have planned to do today, I planned this morning. When I say that I will do something tomorrow, I am faking it. I am lying. Tomorrow will not happen. And, though it is a very nice surprise when I wake up each morning, how many mornings will I have to live through to realize that tomorrow can be expected to show up for me?"

Although, I had finally spoken my insanity aloud, I did not feel better.

"You should talk to someone about this."

"Dude, I am the crazy one. And, even I know, that is what I am doing now, talking about it."

"Not to me. Don't talk to me about it. I can't help you. I don't know how. I can't even guess at what to say. I can't even guess at how you feel."

"Yeah, okay." Who could?

"You need to talk to someone else, a professional."

"Great. I'll do that, then."

He looked at me out of the corner of his eye. "When?"

I laughed, though nothing at all was funny.

"Tomorrow."

(Note, from the Me in Tomorrow: I have not decided, yet, if anyone other than myself will read these words. It is my story, after all, and I do not know if telling it will help anyone else. But, if you do read this, and if you ever feel that your friends or family cannot understand what you are going through, or that they don't have the resources to help, then seek out a professional. And, if the professional doesn't help, then find another one. You are worth more than any stigma, in your mind or in the minds of others. I did not follow my friend's advice, and my experience was much harder than it had to be.)

Because of the nightmares, for a couple of weeks, I took to drinking at night. I was not trying to ease or escape my pain, and I was not to attempting to relax. I wanted to sleep, for just one night, all the way through, without dreaming of the night everything disappeared except the sounds of my neighbors screaming.

It did not work. That never works. Drinking made the nightmares worse, I presume because it was harder to wake up from them. Instead of waking up in the middle of every night, crying, I would wake, curled up in a corner, screaming into a pillow, sobbing and hyperventilating. All my other symptoms, including panic attacks and flashbacks, worsened as well, and the alcohol-induced-sleep trial was short-lived. It had been a bad idea.

Due to my friend's honest helplessness in the face of my emotional storm, I looked up "trauma-induced psychological disorders." In my research, I read a list of PTSD symptoms and when I finished reading, I said two words.

"Oh, shit."

Terms on the computer screen were frighteningly alive in my life. Flashbacks, nightmares, a sense of a foreshortened future, hypervigilance, sleep disturbances, irritability, feelings of betrayal, helplessness, guilt, disconnection, and anxiety interrupted the life I was trying to rebuild.

I did not want to admit the possibility of mild post-traumatic stress disorder, and I had no intention of being diagnosed with it. I was aware that I had been psychologically damaged, though I just referred to my problems as "tornado-brain". The problem must be actively handled. I could not ignore it and hope it went away on its own. Time, alone, does not heal all wounds. I was in trouble. The problem was in my mind, and to solve it, I must apply my mind.

When anxiety attacked, I continued to walk it off, and when walking was not enough, I took Crash to the Greenway and we ran. I concentrated on the pounding of my feet, and the fast click of Crash's toenails on the pavement until my labored breathing was no longer caused by panic, but by exertion.

When my sense of helplessness was overwhelming, I referred to a line I had once read. "My head may think, and my heart may feel, but my hands will work always." I worked on the Normalcy Project with a survivalist's obsession that may have become unhealthy if the project had been endless.

I spoke of hope and faith often, because despite the hopelessness that tornado-brain insisted upon, I tried not to allow that feeling to affect my behavior. Hope was real. I trusted God. That was reality and reality was what it was, despite how I felt about it. I could not trust my feelings, and I spoke of hope and faith, not only to remind my friends about reality, but to continually remind myself.

I failed nearly as often as I tried. I tried to learn to forgive myself, not only for the failures, but for the feelings that created those very challenges. And, I failed at that too, sometimes, but I just tried again.

When my emotional response to a situation was avoidance, I chased that challenge as if my life depended on it, and considered such acts as an unwritten addendum to the

Normalcy Project. Often, it took several aborted attempts, ending in tears and the determination to do better next time.

It took three tries to buy a Christmas wreath for the Sequel. It seemed a simple errand, and for normal people, it would be. I wandered the aisles, looking at various wreaths, thinking, "No, this is not the one I want. I want one that is exactly right for my family. No, this one is too fancy. This one is pretty, but not quite right."

When I realized what I was actually looking for, my heart ruptured, yet again. My son and I had made our wreath for the original Home's first Christmas, together. In poverty, we had to improvise its creation for the most part. That cheap wreath, festively cobbled together with ancient ribbon, staples, a shoelace, love and laughter grew uglier and more ratty-looking over the next decade. I adored it. It was our history.

I realized, not only was I looking for a wreath that resembled that family project, but that the unconscious task was obviously hopeless. No store would carry a ten-year-old homemade wreath that appeared to have a bad case of mange. It was ridiculous to be so upset. If I asked, James would make another wreath with me, as hideous as I wanted. But, the minor loss of our Christmas wreath, coupled with yet another reminder that we had lost everything else, was too much. I left my cart in the holiday aisle, abandoned my shopping, and fled the store.

I have always had the tendency to shut down in times of stress but I knew, now, that communication and connection was key. As I could no longer write to work through my feelings, I was forced to learn to talk openly, instead. I discovered the need to be careful of how, and with whom, I communicated. Some friends focused on the negative. Most truly needed to believe that I was okay, and they could not handle that I could be okay, and yet, not okay. Others put a timeframe on my grief, set their own milestones on my behalf, and could not understand that my normalcy was a process, not a destination. There were those who did not want to talk about my hurts at all, and those who wanted to talk about it incessantly. For many, by the time I reached a point where I could even begin dealing with the effects of the disaster, the statute of limitations had already expired. I had coped so well initially, and they assumed that was the end of it, instead of the beginning.

None of this was anyone's fault, simply a result of personality characteristics (including my own), and complete lack of experience in these matters (including my own).

I had a select group of friends who I could turn to during this time, "Recovery", as the uninitiated call it. These people did not have any answers. But, these friends did what few others could.

They loved me, not as the person I had been, but for the person I was becoming. They loved me during that process of becoming who I would be. And, that is hard. My friends did not want to accept that I would never be the same, any more than I did. But, they tried because that is what Love does.

They listened when I talked, and tried to understand when I did not.

They showed up when I needed help, and tried to understand when I needed to do some things on my own.

They refused to judge, or demand that I feel a certain way.

They allowed me to work through things in my own manner, even when that manner included standing in the rain during an entire thunderstorm, raging back at the raging wind, just because I was so terribly afraid.

They gave me all the time I needed.

They remained available, without expectation and without condition, as long as I needed them.

This is all it takes. The right answers are not required. Avoiding people who are grieving a loss because you do not know what to say to them is an understandable reaction, and it is both unfair and unkind. However, in offering condolences, the phrase "I know exactly how you feel" is always inappropriate. Chances are, you have not lived the trauma, you have only seen it, and there is a world of difference. Even if you have suffered a seemingly similar loss, no two people are identical in feelings or reactions, and though empathy is love, that particular phrase is presumptuous, self-serving, and unhelpful.

An example of what does work is this. A friend let me know that she would be thinking of, and praying for me, every day. She admitted that she did not know what to say to me, or do for me, but was available for anything. She deliberately made it clear that she knew I had a lot going on, and ordered me to never worry about returning her messages, unless I had time and wanted to talk. She would never be offended when I did not respond. Many people said that, actually. In the case of this friend, it was true.

Without fail, every morning for a very long time, I received a text message, brimming with love and thoughtfulness, and that text told me that someone, before dawn, was already thinking of me, praying for me, and had not forgotten me. It was always the exact same message.

That text read, "Hello."

CHAPTER TWENTY-TWO

They Call It Recovery

"Blossom by blossom, the spring begins."

- Algernon Charles Swinburne

The tornado's trail and my bulldozing work had left
my yard stony and barren of life. I dug thousands of rocks,
by hand, from the dirt of my acre. During the dry summer,
my land was a desert, and when it rained, it was a mud pit.

The summer days of 2011 melted in one-hundred-degree
temperatures. I walked the dusty wastelands, back and
forth, and section by section. This time I walked, not merely
to preserve my sanity, but to go with handfuls of grass seed,
scattering them, as I paced. I could merely scatter the seeds.
They must take root, sprout, and grow themselves. I
covered my seeds with straw to protect them from the wind.

I was thinking of wind protection as a silly activity. Mister Twister had already taught me, too well, that the wind cared nothing for me, or my precious seeds. The wind would carry them wherever it willed.

A warm breeze blew, as I shook clumps of straw to pieces, and I paused to wipe dirt and straw from my face. I took a breath of heated air, wondering exactly what temperature oxygen must attain to combust the straw bits in my lungs.

Seed, straw, breathe. Scatter, cover, smother. I felt like an order of Waffle House hash browns. I wasted precious energy on a smile at my own silly joke.

The smile faded when I glanced up the street. Three invisible houses up my street, a news van parked. The cameraman set up, to get the best shot of three homes-in-progress and several empty lots. My life had been reduced to a story, complete with a solemn, pitying voice-over about the poor victims setting up replacement lives, to entertain all those viewers securely at home; the community who was helpful, kind, and sacrificing a few months ago, a community to whom I would forever be grateful.

Nevertheless, this community of sympathizers had already returned to their everyday lives, and they would watch a news stories with their own memories. For just a moment, I hated those who remembered.

They would remember because they had the option to forget. While my family and those like us, never would. However, I owed those viewers so much, so I swallowed the bitterness. It tasted like dirt and straw. I must try to forgive them the forgetting.

The media referred to my everyday life as "Recovery", as if the longing for my original life, the unrecoverable loss of what I had loved, as well as who I had been, was an addiction that could be cured by time and twelve steps.

CHAPTER TWENTY-THREE

Sunburn and Feathers

"I see the storm coming and I know that His hand is in it."

- Abraham Lincoln

God gave me my land. It was an unconditional gift, freely given and gladly accepted. However, Mister Twister had ripped my security away so suddenly, that I deeply felt the need to retrieve my sense of power from the memory of its destruction.

I needed to make the land feel like it was mine, again. I needed to stake my claim. There was only one way to do that and I needed to do this part alone.

The summer after catastrophe, the temperatures reached, and maintained, over one-hundred degrees. By this time, most of the volunteers had returned to their lives and, in an empty neighborhood, I had the privacy to do what needed done, alone. I raked away what seemed millions of rocks from my acre of Promised Land, leveled the torn ground with a shovel, and dug up the stump-corpses of my lovely former shade trees. I taught myself how to use a chainsaw, and somehow maintained possession of all my body parts. I bought a sledgehammer, and wielded it, busting my concrete porch, which the wind had relocated to the center of my front yard, into chunks small enough to bury. Once the Sequel arrived, I planted grass, and built my flowerbed.

My friends offered to help, and I stubbornly declined. My son insisted on showing up and pitching in whenever he could, but he had school and band practice, so I had my alone time to work, and pray.

I carried cases of water and Gatorade in the trunk of my car and stayed hydrated, but it was miserable work. I remembered, pre-tornado, saying that I wanted to get a tan in the summer.

"Thanks, God," I muttered into the shimmering heat, "but, I meant I planned to hang out at the river." I uselessly toweled sweat away and grabbed my water bottle. It was too hot. I needed to quit. But, it wouldn't cool off anytime soon, and the work needed to be completed. I was in a race to Normalcy against Old Man Winter and I planned to give him a run for his money. I could not afford a break. As I thought this, a cool breeze blew and I was refreshed by it. I could work a little longer. I glanced up as I drank, and I was being watched.

A white bird perched on the new power lines, cocking his head to stare at me.

"Hey, little guy, are you supervising?"

Then, I did a double take, and looked hard at the bird. It was a dove. At the sight of it, the memory of a dear friend who had passed away years ago entered my mind. I have no reason to connect this type of bird and that loved person, but the connection stuck, so I presumed the dove was male, and I called it by his name.

The dove and I watched each other, and then I shrugged. I went back to work, and he continued to supervise.

As the hot days wore on and I wore out, I worked. Often, the exertion and heat got to me, and I prayed for a moment's relief so I could continue. At those times, a cool breeze would blow briefly, though it never blew directly in my face, and my winged supervisor arrived on it. Every time I looked up, he was looking at me. After the Sequel was built, but not yet available for habitation, he moved his perch to the roof, where he could supervise my backyard work, too.

One day, I had enough. I was exhausted. My muscles did not just ache. They throbbed. I noticed that I had stopped sweating and knew I had gotten myself into trouble. I had failed to drink enough water that hot day, I was dehydrated, and I suddenly felt very sick. I dropped my rock-rake and sat in the dirt in my backyard. There was a bottle of water in the car, which my body absolutely needed, but I could not move to fetch it. My little breeze blew softly, but not even that got me off the ground. I was finished. A small shadow moved on the ground before me, and I looked up to see what cast it.

The dove's attack knocked me over. His wings beat my face and head, and I covered my face with one arm, flailing wildly with the other. I was screaming, an embarrassingly girly, high-pitched "Eeeeek!" After several long seconds, he landed on the ground a couple of feet away and cocked his head at me.

"What the hell? Jeremy!"

The bird cocked his head the other way, and flew to perch on my rake, lying nearby.

"No," I told him, "No. I'm dying. I can't work today. I'm calling in or turning in my notice. I have not decided which one."

The dove furiously flapped his wings in my direction, and that got me on my feet. I glared at the little bird, as I picked a white feather out of my hair, "Fine, little boss-man. I'm just going to get my water, and then back to work."

I turned away, and then looked back to remark, "To be a symbol of peace, you are a little asshole."

He lifted his little, white tail and crapped on my rake.

CHAPTER TWENTY-FOUR

Counting the Cost

"The pupil dilates in darkness and in the end finds light, just as the soul dilates in misfortune, and in the end finds God."

–Victor Hugo

During a tour of the new Sequel, an old friend exclaimed over how pretty it was, brand new compared to the original, beloved, but run-down home.

"This is much nicer than my place. I wish I had gotten that insurance settlement to get something like this. You are so lucky to get this for pretty much nothing." The words did not hurt me much, but the tone of jealousy stung. She did not know just what she wished for, and I prayed she never got it.

I muttered, "Well, I paid the price for it."

"How much is it worth? I mean, how much, exactly, did it cost you?"

I knew she wanted a dollar amount, but the "pretty much nothing" I had paid, and was still paying, was so much more than money.

"Exactly? Thirty-four years of my life. That's what it cost me."

She opened her mouth, and I interrupted. "I know what you meant. I hope you never have to know what I mean. Go home, and feel lucky for what remains to you, and of you."

My home had disappeared. My life, as I knew it, had ended. My heart was shredded. My mind betrayed me. Even my hair had turned gray. Someone sent me a greeting card, which read, "Right now, you're in the place between the way things were, and the way things are yet to be… and that's the place of Hope."

Hope, the thing with feathers that perches in the soul, sometimes seemed a vulture, patiently watching me crawl along through my Wasteland. I wandered the in-between land on the borders of who I was and who I might become like a ghost haunting my own life.

Still.

I kept the salvageable items from my original life: a single coffee cup, a copper vase, a wooden box, and a globe with a tornado-crack through my state. I filled a shadowbox with small items belonging to Home, the Former: a single, filthy page from James' baby book, and one from his yearbook, a birthday candle used once for my boy's fifth birthday, a palm sized chunk of concrete that had once been part of my front porch, a larger chunk of bedroom drywall and my house keys.

Each of these items had once been an overlooked piece of my life. I paid no attention to them. I used the keys, and I dusted the vase with no clue that, one day, they would be on display as All That Remained.

I missed the capacity to take things for granted. But, that capacity had been replaced with a larger capacity for gratitude.

My former home, and original life, had been full of stuff. My tendency to hoard had disappeared in the wind, and been replaced by a much simpler, minimalist existence.

My independent nature had not quite vanished, but it was tempered by the knowledge that when I became instantly homeless, love sheltered me. I did not have a pot to piss in and was unable to find any of my windows to throw it out. Everything I now owned, even the clothes on my back and the shoes on my feet, was a gift.

The life I knew, and a good part of the self I had created for thirty-four years, is gone forever. I replace those years with every single day that I have left. I fill each of them with as much life and love as I can pack into a day. This, too, has been a trade.

Whenever I drive past a certain spot on the bypass, my heart pipes up plaintively, "I still miss Bruce" and I reply kindly,

"I know. Hush." I continue to battle panic attacks, and fear thunderstorms. These terrors are also gifts, because each reminds me that my sense of power and self-control is an illusion. The nightmares and flashbacks occasionally stop by to visit me, and those visitors never call ahead. They remind me that I will never become who I once was, and I practice forgiving myself for wanting to. As often as it takes, I come to terms with an event that, against my will, became part of who I am. Blessed and highly favored, no matter how much it still hurts.

There was a night when I sat on a couch that had belonged to someone else until I had need of one, in the miracle of homecoming known as The Sequel. I looked at the handful of garden-variety household goods, my prized possessions, the memories I could still hold in my hands.

I thought on what had been taken from me, and my heart still ached for Before, but that was natural and I was learning not to fight it. I thought on the losses that were not either replaced or transformed into something different, but still good.

I sat there on someone else's couch and counted those irretrievable losses, what the tornado had cost me. I counted them on my fingers and I used both hands.

Then, I began counting blessings. I ran out of fingers, and had to go outside and use the stars.

CHAPTER TWENTY-FIVE

Life, the After-Party

"Part of you did die that night. Life, as you knew it, is over. But, after a show is finished, there is generally one hell of an after-party."

-Carol Smith, 2011

A couple days prior to my thirty-fifth birthday, I flipped through thirty-four pages on a legal pad. Each sheet was filled, on both sides, with stuff to do, stuff to replace, options to look into and every single to-do item that must be completed in order for my family to begin a normal life, again. It was fourteen days shy of a full year, and those items had been crossed off, while the pages, themselves, became dirty, torn, wrinkled, and stained with time, sweat, tears, and a little blood.

"James!"

My son and his friend came into the kitchen. I held up the legal pad, titled "Project Normalcy", my constant companion for three hundred and fifty-one days. My child raised an eyebrow. He did not have to ask what it was, as Project Normalcy had really been both our companion for three hundred and fifty-one days.

"Is it finished?"

I flung the legal pad into the trash, and we all hugged.

"We have to celebrate!"

"We'll have a party. When would you like one?"

"On my birthday, of course!"

I hesitated. The tornado had ruined his last birthday, and I was not sure about focusing on that for this one. We could have two parties, instead.

"No, Mom. My birthday is the anniversary of the tornado, and I want a tornado-themed party, a Screw You, Mister Twister party."

His friend piped up, "We could rent The Wizard of Oz."

James laughed, "And play Twister!"

I cracked up, "How about a house-shaped piñata?"

"We are so twisted!"

"Twisted? Oh, I see what you did there! That's clever."

My beautiful, talented niece created a piñata that looked like my former home. We secretly filled it, not with candy, but with tiny toy people, trees, furniture, and matchbox cars. As a practical joke, with my laughing permission, she lined the inside of the piñata with duct tape so that it would be difficult for the eighteen-year-olds to break.

As a prank a few months before, a friend had left a life-size Grinch on my front porch. I had kept the Grinch, and made use of him for the party. During catastrophe clean up, many people had driven by, slowly, with camera and comments of "This is so cool!" Those jerk sightseers deserved to be symbolized during our celebration. I attached a camera to the Grinch's hand. James' friend, Aaron, made a dunce cap and a sign reading "Hello! I'm a stupid sightseer!"

That party was meant to be a celebration, both of James' birthday and our survival, but it ended up being very therapeutic, in a twisted way. (Yes, I see what I did there. Clever.)

With The Wizard of Oz on TV in the background, I played Twister with my nephews. Rather, being middle-aged and clumsy, I tried to play with them. James and his friends played guitar and sang in his music room, and then went outside and danced in my driveway. Then it was time for the outside party games.

We laughed so hard at the boys' confusion when the duct-tape lined piñata would not break, at first, and then at their comments when it finally did.

"There is nothing but broken junk in it."

"Welcome to the world of a tornado victim!"

James grabbed the busted piñata and announced "Re-enactment!" He spun in circles, as he ran across the street to the now empty lot where most of our former home had landed, calling "Look at me. I'M A TORNADO!" I joined him, laughing, "I want to be a tornado, too", and we played soccer with the house piñata. Then, as with our old house, we cleaned up the mess, giggling over how easy it was the second time. I hummed a few bars of "We're Off to See the Wizard, the Wonderful Wizard of Oz," and we skipped back to the Sequel.

I carried our Sightseer to the front yard, briefly explaining what he signified for our family, though almost all of the boys had helped with disaster clean up, knew what a "sightseer" was, and how each one had injured us. After giving the boys a firm lecture on safety and taking turns, I pointed to the side of the porch, where we had arranged a baseball bat, a machete, a shovel, and other assorted weapon-like instruments. "Take those," I then pointed at our Sightseer, "and destroy him."

The kids offered me first swing. I declined the sweet gesture, as I hurriedly rescued my camera from the doomed Grinch's hand, while all my armed kids circled around us. As I looked at the innocent Grinch, I remembered all of the fools who had driven by the "cool" disaster zone, entertaining themselves with my tragedy.

I kicked the Sightseer, hard in the crotch, and snarled, "How does it feel?" as he flew through the air.

The boys cheered and then fell upon him, tearing him to pieces.

They played baseball with the Sightseer's decapitated head, wore his hat and jacket, and carried his arms around, as trophies. They had a blast, and followed all my safety precautions. The adults watched, laughed, cheered, and thought about the deep pain that the real sightseers had caused every tornado victim.

I walked to where the Sightseer lay, and borrowed my machete from a teenager. I remembered every so-called human who had driven by tragedy for their own amusement, while the real humans, the helpers, slaved in the rubble. I ripped open the pants of the Sightseer's backside with the machete, picked up his decapitated head, and shoved it far up his arse.

As I returned to the porch, a friend called, "How did that feel?"

It felt good. It felt very good.

The kids built a bonfire. My birthday boy emerged from our Sequel, outfitted in an impromptu Mister Twister costume, with the plastic Twister mat as a cape and the spinner as a hat. Those objects ended up in the fire, as we danced and shouted, "Screw you, Mister Twister! We win!"

After the celebration ended and the children went to bed, I sat in the backyard, alone, while the fire burned low, and opened my first beer of the evening.

I considered the life I had lost and I said good-bye to it, again. Good-bye is never all at once, it just comes in little pieces of grief and healing, in great love and overwhelming pain, often in the same moment. Such sorrow is not a journey to the great destination of healing. The path is life, and those two walk hand in hand.

I considered my year of aftermath. I admitted that I had never entirely believed that I could make it through. Not until this very minute, when it was finally over. I had only fought one day at a time, and when a day was too long to handle, I fought an hour at a time, or sometimes, only five minutes at a time. Victory is never all at once, it just comes in little steps forward, and each step is a triumph, even when it doesn't feel like one.

I sipped my icy beer, and it tasted good.

I listened to the sounds of the night, frogs, crickets, and the crackling of the fire. They were all playing my song.

A party guest, just before leaving, had asked me the same old question but with a new tone.

"What are you going to do, now?"

I sat in the young grass beside the smoking remains of a charred Twister game, while I enjoyed the sensation, for the first time since my former life disappeared, of my body slowly relaxing. In the moonlight, the Mama-Tree cast her beautiful, broken shadow across my promised land.

I knew the answer this time.

I inhaled, deeply. I exhaled, slowly. The day after the end of the world had finally ended. Tomorrow was in the air, and I filled my lungs with it.

"What are you going to do, now?"

Rest.

EPILOGUE

Little Phoenix

The phoenix, I once believed, was the epitome of coolness, the beautiful, mythical symbol of rebirth and the strength that the result represented. The phoenix was able to withstand a bit of pain and become someone entirely new. Wouldn't the fire be worth it? I, innocently, thought so.

And, then, in the Spring of 2011, the terrible wind blew- and I became a little phoenix.

The pyre, I have discovered, is not merely painful. It is agonizing and lasts long past the time when the flames die. Does the phoenix know that she will rise again, or does it feel like only death? Does the question even matter? When a creature rises from the ashes, she does not feel special, or wise, or strong- because she is not; she is only streaked with tears, and dirt, and blood.

The new creature knows who she once was; she remembers and misses, of all people, herself. She recalls a girl who she can never be again, and that bereavement resembles someone grieving a lost love, not a woman still wearing her own skin. The empty spaces waiting to be filled are still a void.

Her head is high, not in pride, but in self-preservation. If she falls to the ground in despair, then she will die a second death, for no reason and with no resurrection. The new wings spread to escape the hurt, but where would she fly? Consumed fire in determined eyes is her love for her friends. Wounds so deep that she does not know where pain ends and she begins, they cannot be eased by sharing, only spread. Having lived through the unthinkable, spreading that pain to those who care enough to share it seems unfathomable.

"So different now." "Nice tan." "The gray hair suits you." She accepts these statements with as much poise as unease can muster, because what they mean is this. In a time when her heart, her sense of safety, her own personal little refuge has been destroyed in a moment; when everything is strange, and she is desperate for something she knows, not even the mirror holds anything familiar. Dear companions look at her differently because they have seen her through the fire. And, she sees her world as a foreign land, a forced paradigm shift, all still blurry through the residual smoke.

Does the phoenix want her plain, ugly, battered, old self back? Through the sheer gratitude of being alive, of being shown love in abundance, of miracles, of blessings uncountable and of the peace within her storm...does the new one ever look up at the stars and pray, "God? Just between you and me, I really miss my life"? Yes.

And God, who once answered a devastated woman's cry of "Jesus, if you love me, take it back," with "No."

God, who responded to a pitifully whispered "Why have You forsaken me?" with such an outpouring of miracles and human kindness, that the obvious answer was "I haven't."

God, who heard a broken woman's accusation "If this is for Your glory, then You screwed up. I am not strong enough."

and was not offended, but answered, softly and lovingly, with "I never asked you to be strong enough, only to remember that I AM."

There is a difficult, sarcastic little sinner, who is in front of her God-given home (affectionately known as "The Sequel"), sitting on her family-built front porch. She says evening prayers on her own personal promised land every night, dealing with ashes that are still warm, and coming to terms with a beloved, destroyed life. She grieves, not for things, but for moments. She busies herself putting her past, and a good chunk of herself, to rest and practices drawing blueprints, in pencil, for tomorrow. Sometimes, she cries, "It still hurts." God does not reply, "It will end soon." Instead, He unfailingly answers, "I am still with you."

Why was my home destroyed? The life I planted, almost a decade ago, torn up by the roots? The woman I learned to respect, if not always like, sent to walk through Limbo and return home as a stranger? I'm just beginning to consider asking those questions and, already, the answer doesn't matter.

There is a stranger in my mirror, now. She doesn't look like me, think like me, feel like me, and only acts like me when she remembers to. She is formed by fire and wind.

Was the fire that arrived in that wind worth it? Not yet, but I am starting to think it will be.

Do I feel sorry for that mythical bird? Oh, terribly.

Will I ever be me again? I doubt it. And, that's all good.

It was the stranger, this Phoenix, who stood as me in my backyard, her first night on the Promised Land. She looked silently, with more gratitude than I have ever known, at the Sequel. She stared with new eyes, as if she had never seen lights in the windows of a home.

The Phoenix then turned to face the brokenness marking the path that my destruction took. She raised both middle fingers and screamed her version of hallelujah, the tones in her voice blending in equal measures of sorrow, rage, and secondhand triumph. "Screw you, Mister Twister! My God is *bigger*!"

"Never to suffer would have been never to have been blessed."

-Edgar Allan Poe

THE END.

(Just kidding. It is really the beginning. Every day is, for me and for you. So, how about this, instead?)

AMEN.

ACKNOWLEDGEMENTS

Mom, Dad, Joyce, Brian, Melody, Haley, Madison, Carmen, Marty and Erica- through all of my messes, you never gave up on me. I am so blessed to be a member of the best family ever. I don't say it enough: I love each of you so very much.

James- Your constant encouragement and eye for detail have been essential in the creation of this book. You are my ultimate pride, my truest love, and my deepest joy. Not only in this part of our story, but in every single chapter of my life, you are my hero. I love you more than life, dearest one.

Every family member, by blood and by bond- All my love.

ACKNOWLEDGEMENTS

CS, TS, & DJ- for sharing the love of our Starfish. I was fortunate, many years ago, to be welcomed as part of your family, and I am blessed that your stories and mine are intertwined.

Leigh, the daughter of my heart, you are my editor, my oh-so-talented cover artist, my cheerleader and ego-repairer, and most of all, my friend. You have become such a huge, wonderful part of my life. I aspire to be more like you. I love you, Little Dog.

Bobby Rayfield and Ryan Locklear of Inherent Records, Mike York, Preston Parris & company- for replacing the music. Mother Nature stole from my child, and you, dearest of selfless gentlemen, gave it back to him.

Beki- for insisting on salvaging my secrets, protecting them, and for performing a truly miraculous resurrection on my lucky bamboo plant. I could not ask for a more wonderful Other Me.

Misty, my sister– for showing up in my life, weathering my storm, and never, ever, ever leaving. You teach me how to be courageous, every single day.

The angels of Dixie Day Spay, Community Veterinary Hospital, Constant Companion, Black Fox Pet Resort, Dee, Greg, Kevin, Travis, Amanda, Mike, Stacey, Beth, Betti, Dr. G, Cottonwood Farm, and each employee of Lowe's Home Improvement #649– it takes a village to fend for a pack of homeless, unruly mutts. Thank you for building that village of compassion for my furry babies.

Sarah, I cannot thank you for everything you have done for me. "Thanks" just isn't enough. Your wisdom, your compassion, your encouragement, your friendship, and your faith are a true inspiration. Your "Gift to God" is, also, a gift to everyone else. From "the empress of nutsdom"

Jonathan and Joan, whose kind words have so often been a balm to my soul— I would never have told this story without you.

Cindy, Larry, Shadey, Drew, Curtis, & James— When my heart was rubble, you serenaded outside my window. I could not have survived Limbo without each of you pouring your love into my wounds. Also, I need to say this to you: I just lost The Game.

Members of local churches: Rock Point Church, First Baptist Church, New Hope Church, Waterville Baptist Church, Bradley Baptist Association, and so many more. Thank you for loving thy neighbors.

ACKNOWLEDGEMENTS

Stephanie Morris, disaster coordinator and friend extraordinaire, and each member of the churches in Florida, who traveled so far to be God's hands and feet (& chainsaw)- Rivertown Community Church (Pastor Paul Smith) in Blountstown, Florida, Altha Church of God (Pastor Alan Nichols), and The Bridge (Pastor Gailand Gay). Thank you so much.

Employees of Lowe's #2593 in Southbend, Indiana, Lowe's #0140 in Issaquah, WA, and Lowe's Corporate Office departments- I still have the cards you sent and I remember the kindness you showed to a stranger.

Lake Forest Middle School- for searching out an old copy of my child's yearbook. You gave a piece of my son's history back to him, and that meant so much to both of us.

ACKNOWLEDGEMENTS

Bradley Central High School, Cleveland Animal Control, Bradley County Road Dept., Bradley County Sheriff's Dept., Cleveland Utilities, Bradley Cleveland Emergency Services, Red Cross, Salvation Army, & on & on & on.

Those who drove the streets of disaster, not to sightsee, but to look for people they could help in their own "little" way. People like Paul Gates and his wife, Patti, who washed my salvaged laundry so that I could have my own clothing. Such little acts are huge.

Each friend, stranger, volunteer, and organization who offered aid to my family- Even if I could thank you individually and personally, I do not own the words to express my gratitude. I am not sure if those words exist. I can never repay your kindness but I shall never forget it.

I love you all.

Works Cited

Unless indicated otherwise*, all non-Biblical quotes are considered to be in the public domain.

Alcott, Louisa May. Little Women. United States: Roberts Brothers, 1869. Print.

Alighieri, Dante. "The Divine Comedy" in The Harvard Classics. Trans. Henry F. Cary. Vol. XX. New York: P.F. Collier & Son, 1909-14. Print.

Austen, Jane. Sense and Sensibility. London: Appleby &, 1939. Print.

Baum, L. Frank. The Wonderful Wizard of Oz. Chicago: George M. Hill, 1900. Print.

Dickinson, Emily. The Complete Poems of Emily Dickinson. Boston: Little, Brown, 1924. Print.

Dostoyevsky, Fyodor, and Frederick Whishaw. Crime and Punishment. London: J.M. Dent & Sons, 1911. Print.

Hugo, Victor. Les Misérables. Trans. Isabel Florence Hapgood. New York: T.Y. Crowell, 1887. Print.

Ketcham, Henry. The Life of Abraham Lincoln. New York: A.L. Burt, 1901. Print.

*Larche, Jimmy. 13-Foot Coffins: Because Giants Were Meant to Be Slain. 2011. Print. Reprinted with Permission.

London, Jack. The Star Rover. New York: Macmillan, 1915. Print.

MacDonald, George. Unspoken Sermons: Third Series. London: Longmans, Green, 1889. Print.

WORKS CITED

Marcus Aurelius. "The Meditations of Marcus Aurelius" in The Harvard Classics. Trans. George Long. Part 3 ed. Vol. II. New York: P.F. Collier & Son, 1909-1914. Print.

Melville, Herman. Moby Dick; Or, The Whale. London: Richard Bentley, 1851. Print.

Nietzsche, Friedrich. Thus Spake Zarathustra. Trans. Alexander Tille. London: Union, 1899. Print.

Poe, Edgar Allan. "Mesmeric Revelation" in Tales of Edgar A. Poe. New York: Wiley and Putnam, 1845. Print.

Shakespeare, William. "The Tragedy of King Richard the Second" in The Oxford Shakespeare: The Complete Works of William Shakespeare. London: Oxford UP, 1914. Print.

Stowe, Harriet Beecher. Uncle Tom's Cabin; Or, Life Among the Lowly. Boston: Houghton, Mifflin, 1889. Print.

Swinburne, Algernon Charles. "Chorus from Atalanta" in The Oxford Book of English Verse. Ed. Arthur Thomas Quiller-Couch. Oxford: Clarendon, 1900. Print.

Thoreau, Henry David. "On Walking" in Essays: English and American. Vol. XXVIII. New York: P.F. Collier & Son, 1910. Print.

Vonnegut, Kurt. 2BR02B. Auckland: Floating, 1962. Print.

About the Author:

(This bit seems overkill. After all, the entire book is about the author.)

Rebecca is a writer and tornado survivor, but God has involved her in other roles where she, also, receives more than she gives. She is a mother, grandmother, daughter, sister, and friend. She is a silly girl, an animal rescuer, and an active member of the human race.

When Rebecca is not immersed in wholehearted servitude to the best little boy in the universe, her time is divided between scribbling and fulfilling the needs of one too many rescue pets.

She is addicted to coffee, nicotine, and studying whichever random subjects strike her fancy. Rebecca is created entirely of flaws, stitched together with good intentions and the grace of God.

Thanks for reading!

If you would like to order a paperback copy or e-book, for yourself, as a gift, or simply to invest in Rebecca's coffee addiction:

www.rebeccascrivens.weebly.com

Contact the author and let her know what you think of The Day After the End of the World, join her private mailing list, and be among the first to become aware of her new books, or just say hello:

Email: tornadochick2011@gmail.com